The King Ranch Quarter Horses

Anita Chica, one of the great show mares raised by the King Ranch, ridden by Richard M. Kleberg, Jr. She is doing what all King Ranch Quarter Horses are bred to do—working cattle without any special directions from her rider.

THE KING RANCH QUARTER HORSES

And Something of the Ranch and the Men That Bred Them

By Robert Moorman Denhardt

University of Oklahoma Press

Norman

By Robert Moorman Denhardt

The Quarter Horse (3 volumes, Amarillo, 1941–50)
The Horse of the Americas (Norman, 1947)
Quarter Horses: A Story of Two Centuries (Norman, 1967)
The King Ranch Quarter Horses (Norman, 1970)

International Standard Book Number: 0–8061–0924–6

Library of Congress Catalog Card Number: 73–123340

"I feel that our effort with the Quarter Horse is a very important one, and if we possibly can, we should keep the thing alive. In my mind, Quarter Horses are just as important on the ranch as the hardy strains that we have developed from the Brahman cattle. The Quarter Horse should be on every ranch. I think that one thing we should stress more about these horses is the fact that they are the hardiest of all strains of horses under range conditions."

Robert J. Kleberg, Jr.
(Letter to the author, October 6, 1942)

Foreword

It has been in my mind to make this book somewhat less than a history of the King Ranch but considerably more than just the story of a great horse. To paraphrase my old friend "Pancho" Dobie, I shall sometimes be riding alongside the Klebergs and sometimes picking my way afoot, tracking down some horse that came from outside the confines of the ranch. One soon finds that the motivating force behind the formation of the King Ranch Quarter Horses was one man, Robert J. Kleberg, Jr.

This then is a story of horses and people. Not all horses or all people, but some very special ones. The characters in the story are divided between those native to the Santa Gertrudis and the inquilines who crossed the fence and took root. The Klebergs and the mare Brisa are examples of those bred on the ranch. Dr. J. K. Northway and the Old Sorrel are individuals who came to the ranch and found a permanent home. I hope to show how these individuals, human and equine, interreacted and how the hand of Bob Kleberg guided the action.

Texas cowmen do not suffer from an inferiority complex, nor are they uncertain in action. They are not and do not consider themselves laborers or grubbers in the soil. Nevertheless, few workers have ever labored harder than the men of the King Ranch.

The cattleman is basically a cavalier, in the true meaning of that word. As a man on horseback he has ever been a stirrup above the man on foot.

If America has ever had a feudal lord, it has certainly been the cattle rancher. He has governed his range principality with all the vigor of a medieval lord —but with one big difference. He has not expected his *vaqueros* to do any work that he could not do, whether riding, roping, cutting, or branding.

Such are the Klebergs. As the saying goes, they would charge hell with a bucket of water if it would serve the ranch.

I am beholden to many people for this book, and I am sorry that I cannot personally mention each one of them. My obligation to some is great; for example, to the entire King Ranch personnel, all of whom went out of their way to help me. The time I spent on the Norias Division of the ranch with Robert J. Kleberg, his daughter, Helenita, and Ed Durham primed the pump. I had not seen Helen since 1940, when she was a girl, and the visits we shared and the suggestions she and her father offered did much to set the pattern for the book.

Two men who gave many hours of their valuable time trying to ensure the accuracy of the account were Richard M. Kleberg and Dr. J. K. Northway. Dick Kleberg personally escorted me to different divisions of the ranch so that I could see the ranch horses at work. He never refused a request for assistance of any kind, and he saw to it that I had everything I needed. Doc Northway, the internationally known veterinarian of the ranch, put up with constant questioning and checked innumerable facts. No one could have been more helpful. He always had advice, counsel, and a storehouse filled with memories and information, all available at any hour of the day or night. We renewed a friendship that had begun almost thirty years before, and I all but became a member of the Northway family. It would be understandable if his gracious wife was relieved when the summers passed and I went on my way. The hours I spent in Doc's home and at his office, and the fishing adventures we shared at the reservoir near the veterinary barns, played an important part in making this book a joy to write.

A few others deserve special mention; for example, Tom Lea, whose volumes on the King Ranch contributed so much to this work and whose advice was invaluable. Whatever import the book has owes much to his artistry. Gail Boon, the capable manager of the Quarter Horse records, is another special person. Her natural love of horses and her familiarity with the ranch Quarter Horses made her a real ally. She too devoted many hours to checking the manuscript for accuracy. John Cypher helped with pictures and general historical data. Bill Kiel showed me many varieties of ranch wildlife. And Leonard Stiles was always ready for any venture.

Other capable persons who made many contributions to the book are Helen McFarland, secretary to Dr. Northway; Virginia Bentley, assistant to John Cypher; and Ruth Florence, who could find anything in the files downtown.

Persons not associated with the ranch assisted and encouraged me in many ways. Savoie Lottinville, director emeritus of the University of Oklahoma Press, first suggested that I write such a book back in 1949, soon after the Press published *The Horse of the Americas*. He made many invaluable suggestions. Loyd Jinkens and Ernest Lane were willing to talk King Ranch Quarter Horses whenever we could get together. John Almond, who grew up with some of the outstanding South Texas Quarter Horse families, was particularly helpful. He contributed some of the early foundation mares to the ranch and knows the history of almost every South Texas Quarter Horse. Roy Davis, editor of the *Quarter Horse Journal*, was also ready to leave his desk any time and talk horse over a cup of coffee. When a question arose that the American Quarter Horse Association could help answer, he was my principal source of information.

To those mentioned above and to the many others who contributed, I am most grateful. I hope they like the book.

ROBERT M. DENHARDT

Arbuckle, California

Contents

Illustrations

XIII

Map

The King Ranch Quarter Horses

Introduction

EQUUS, a primitive horse of the Glacial period, once lived in America. For a number of reasons he did not survive, and there were no horses in America when the Spaniards arrived in the fifteenth century.

The first horses to arrive on the mainland were sixteen steeds brought to Veracruz, Mexico, in 1519 by Hernán Cortés. When Cortés had conquered Mexico, he sent to Cuba for livestock to plenish his lands. It was not long before there were many stock ranches in New Spain, as Mexico was called. Cortés led the way by establishing large horse- and cattle-breeding establishments in Oaxaca. When the silver mines of Zacatecas were opened in the last half of the sixteenth century, the resulting prosperity and increased business created a demand that resulted in the breeding and pasturing of thousands of horses and mules in the high plains north of Mexico City.

In 1562, Francisco de Ibarra became governor of a new province in northwestern Mexico called Nueva Vizcaya (now the states of Durango, Chihuahua, Sinaloa, Sonora, and southern Coahuila). The Indians in the region had never been conquered when Ibarra moved in with missionaries and settlers. Before long, however, the fertile river bottoms and broad meadows were dotted with horses and cattle. In 1586, Diego de Ibarra branded 33,000 head of cattle and Rodrigo del Río branded 42,000 head. Such numbers, which indicate the extent of the livestock industry, required many horses.

3

Sinaloa was also stocked with horses when Ibarra took settlers and livestock west over the Sierra Madres. The main settlement was at Topia, but he established another one on the Río del Fuerte, which was later destroyed in an Indian attack. When Pedro de Montoyo re-established the settlement twenty years later, he was warmly received by the natives. Montoyo was amazed to see great numbers of horses and cattle peacefully grazing in the river meadows. According to his report on the expedition, the animals abandoned when the settlement was attacked had increased to 10,000 head. This story was repeated many times along the frontier.

In the early 1600's Juan de Oñate established ranches in New Mexico. Thirty years later it was common to see Indians in the territory riding horseback. Father Eusebio Kino, a Jesuit missionary, established Pimería Alta, and by 1700 there were twenty missions and settlements in the region, as far north as Arizona and New Mexico, all raising horses.

Again the story was repeated when horses were introduced into Texas. In 1665, Fernando de Azcué collected soldiers and horses in Saltillo and Monterrey and crossed the Río Grande. Many missions and ranches were established in Texas during the next few years. Tejas Indians attacked the settlements in 1673, and the Spaniards were forced to retreat to Coahuila, abandoning their horses, their cattle, and their cultivated lands.

The Spaniards eventually moved back into Texas. Alonzo de León made an expedition in 1687, marching over what was to be King Ranch land. As far as can be told, he was the second European to cross the region; Cabeza de Vaca had been the first.[1] Alonzo de León was surprised to see mounted Indians, although, in view of developments elsewhere, it should not have been unexpected. He made several trips northward, taking five hundred to a thousand horses on each trip. Livestock thrived in the area under the supervision of Father Pedro de Villa.

Long before 1700 the American Southwest, from the Pacific to the Sabine River, had been settled and stocked by the Spaniards. From the first the Spanish authorities were aware of the military advantage horses assured

---

1 In 1536, Cabeza de Vaca crossed the Nueces River and, after traveling through the region of the future Rancho de Santa Gertrudis, eventually rejoined his companions in Culiacán, the northern outpost of Sinaloa.

them. Laws were passed in an effort to keep the Indians from learning to ride horses. The Spaniards' fear of mounted Indians was well founded. Both the Spaniards and the Anglo-Americans were brought to a halt when they came face to face with Indian horsemen. The Indian on horseback with his bow and quiver of arrows was a more efficient warrior than a mounted European with a single-shot muzzle-loading musket. The Indian maintained his superiority until the Colt revolver and the repeating rifle gave the white man equality in frontier warfare. Equality did not mean conquest, however, and many more bloody years elapsed before the Indian was finally controlled. Captain Richard King was primarily responsible for pacifying the strip of land between the Río Grande and the Nueces River.

One reason the Spaniards were unsuccessful in their efforts to keep Indians and horses separated was that there were not enough Spaniards to do all the work on the missions and ranches. Of necessity Christianized Indians were put to work as *vaqueros*. When a change of heart or a misunderstanding occurred, the Indian simply rode away, and you may be sure that he had no intention of becoming a pedestrian again. From the herds of horses and cattle found in the region he took what he wanted. Those that escaped wandered away, to become mustangs and longhorns.

Clark Wissler believed that the wild horses were descendants of animals that had escaped from the De Soto, Coronado, or Oñate expeditions. As Francis Haines pointed out, however, the Spaniards rode only stallions, and, no matter how many of them escaped, no progeny could result.[2] Outlying Spanish missions and ranches attacked by Indians and abandoned by the settlers were the true origin of the wild herds.

During the last thirty years of the seventeenth century the Plains Indians enlarged their horse herds in a series of attacks on the northernmost Spanish settlements. Driven south before the fury of the attacks, the settlers took only the barest essentials with them, leaving behind their herds of livestock. In 1697 some element of peace was finally restored by Governor Pedro Rodríguez Cubero, and the settlements were re-established. Nevertheless,

[2] Clark Wissler, "The Influence of the Horse in the Development of Plains Culture," *American Anthropologist,* Vol. XVI, No. 1 (1914); Francis Haines, "Where Did the Plains Indians Get Their Horses?" *American Anthropologist,* Vol. XL, No. 1 (1940).

ranches and villages in New Mexico continued to be attacked by Navahos from the west, Comanches from the north, and Apaches from the south and east, all of whom were generally in search of horses.

During periods of peace Comanches and Yutas (Utes) went to Taos to trade, exchanging skins and captives for European goods and horses. During those early days a group of traders known as *comancheros* carried on a lively trade with the Indians of the plains. Horses and mules were the principal items of trade.

Many years later, when Captain Randolph B. Marcy was mapping the southern half of the Santa Fe Trail from Fort Worth, he mentioned seeing the camps and trails of the *comancheros*. He wrote that certain routes had been followed each year until the trails had become as plain as wagon roads.

The French and English, who came after the Spaniards, also traded with the Indians. When Domingo Ramón was occupying East Texas in 1716, he found the Indians trading horses with the French, and particularly with Louis Juchereau de St. Denis, who was obtaining horses for his French settlements. Ramón was surprised to find that the Indians had considerable quantities of European trade goods, such as knives, guns, and blankets. The French were coming from Natchitoches and, like the English, were trading for horses. The Spaniards never liked this activity in their country, but they were unable to do anything to stop it.

One of the first Anglo-Saxons to gain fame in horse trading in Texas was Philip Nolan. (No doubt some of Nolan's fame rests on Edward Everett Hale's incidental use of his name in "The Man Without a Country.") Nolan's contribution was to demonstrate how easily one could enter and trade in Spanish territory. Nolan led a series of expeditions into Texas. In 1795 he obtained 250 horses in San Antonio. Later, on another trip, he obtained more than 1,000 head. His trading activities became so profitable that he was soon maintaining pasturelands on the Medina and Trinity rivers, where he held and rested the horses on the long trip back to his headquarters in Natchez, Mississippi. There is evidence that he obtained some horses from the area that is now the King Ranch.

The horse that lived in Texas in those days was an individual molded

6

by his environment. Several hundred years of living in Texas had produced in him some admirable characteristics. He had acquired hardihood, self-reliance, endurance, and the ability to live off the country. He did not need to be pampered. Such is the background of the horses which were first used by Captain King and on whose backs the King Ranch was created. They were as resolute and sturdy as the captain himself.

PART I

1. Mesteños and Cimarrones

THE Spaniards living along each side of the Río Grande called the wild horses *mesteños* and the wild cattle *cimarrones*. The *mesteños* were captured for transportation, and the cattle supplied food for people crossing their range. When ranches were established in the country between the Río Grande and the Nueces, the semiferal animals were killed or driven off or found their way into the herds of the settlers. American settlers called the horses mustangs, a corruption of *mesteños*, and they dubbed the wild cattle longhorns, for obvious reasons.

In that wild country unbranded cattle, which were free for the branding, soon came to be called mavericks. Accounts of the origin of the term vary. The explanation credited to Charlie Siringo seems as likely as any to be correct. Siringo, who mavericked on the coast of Texas in 1885, gained lasting fame when he started a new literary trend by writing a cowboy autobiography. According to his account, a stubborn rancher named Maverick decided that since all his neighbors had gone to the trouble of branding their cattle there was no reason for him to do so. He just let the world know that thenceforth all unbranded cattle were his. Soon all wild or unclaimed cattle came to be called mavericks.

Some historians of the early Texas cowman have claimed that all a person needed to get started as a rancher were a rope, an iron, and the nerve to use them. It took much more than that. To begin with, there was no market for

11

mavericks at the time when they were most plentiful. Later, after the wild cattle had become valuable, ranchers were buying land and settling down. These men belonged to a masterful breed, willing and able to protect their land and the surrounding range and the unbranded horses and cattle that lived on it.

When Captain Richard King founded his ranch on Santa Gertrudis Creek, wild cattle and horses abounded. He liked the cattle, but as far as he was concerned the mustangs just ate up the grass. King did not try to use many of the wild horses, preferring to obtain his original cow horses in Mexico.

Mustanging was, however, a profitable sideline for many other ranchers and cowboys in the Nueces strip. Both the Mexican government in Coahuila and the American government in Texas recognized mustanging as a business and passed laws to regulate it. The Texas legislature enacted laws in 1827, 1852, and 1854 designed to control the practice.

The earliest habitations in the land north and east of the Río Grande were primarily horse ranches—if you could call the mustangers' camps ranches. According to Leroy P. Graf, most of the camps were fairly close to the Río Grande, since outlaws and Indians made settlement farther away too dangerous. Graf also observed that the ranchers could not pasture many horses on the plains between the Nueces and the Río Grande because they would have been swept away by the herds of wild horses.[1] Some of these early ranches were owned by businessmen along the border who hired cowboys to run them.

There were still wild horses living on the King Ranch when Robert J. Kleberg, Sr., began managing it. His son, Bob Kleberg, tells the following story that his father told him. Wild horses were so numerous in some places on the ranch that they were eating all the grass, especially around the water holes. Competition with the mustangs was making it very difficult to build up the cattle herds and handle them properly. Moreover, the very presence of the mustangs made the cattle wild. At the same time Kleberg was looking for something that he could sell. At last he decided to get rid of the mustangs

[1] Leroy P. Graf, "Economic History of the Lower Rio Grande Valley," Unpublished Thesis, Harvard University, 1942.

by rounding them up and selling them. He built a large corral, cutting down trees and turning the tops inward to form a funnel-shaped corral. The entrance to the corral was near Tulosa Lake, which the trap surrounded. At that time the lake contained the only good water for miles around, and large numbers of mustangs, wild cattle, and other animals went to it. After the trap was completed and the animals had become accustomed to going in and out of the entrance, Kleberg closed the opening. The first time he did so, he estimated, he and his men trapped at least four thousand head of wild horses. Bob Kleberg believes that it may have been as large a band of wild horses as were ever captured at one time.

Kleberg, Sr., said that after he caught the horses he could not decide how to handle them. He gathered the *vaqueros*, who attempted to drive out the horses, whereupon the mustangs immediately stampeded. Kleberg himself was riding a very strong and powerful horse named Pantalon, a sorrel with four white feet. When Kleberg saw what was happening, he ran in front of the horses and tried to stop them. He had a large quirt with an iron handle with which he actually hit some of the mustangs, but they paid no attention to him. All the horses got away.

It was six months before the horses began to water at the lake again. When Kleberg had captured another large group, he took his men into the trap and drove the horses around and around for several days. During that time the horses had nothing to eat, and the weaker they got the more they accepted handling. Finally the men were able to drive them out of the trap under control. Kleberg sent a trainload of mustangs to Mississippi and Tennessee, trading them for well-bred horses.

2. Captain King Comes to Texas

RICHARD King was born in New York City on July 10, 1824, the son of Irish immigrants. His parents were very poor, and he was apprenticed to a craftsman, but he was unhappy in his new trade. Before long he ran away, stowing aboard the sailing ship *Desdemona*. When he was discovered, the captain liked him and allowed him to remain on the ship as cabin boy. King soon became familiar with the rough but rewarding routine of sea life. From a slender lad of eleven he soon developed into a husky young man.

Richard King liked the Gulf Coast. The warm, balmy air appealed to him after the cold winters of New York. Later, with his captain's permission, he changed ships and signed aboard a shallow-draft steamboat that plied the rivers and shallow waters near the coast. During the next few years he served on several boats, each time securing a better berth. By the time he was nineteen, he was a man to be reckoned with in every respect. He could handle his own in the rough, tough, boisterous seagoing life. In 1843 he met his future partner, Mifflin Kenedy, master of the steamboat *Champion*. By that time King was a pilot—and a good one.

Richard King and Mifflin Kenedy hit it off from the start. It was curious in some ways that they became such good friends. King was outgoing, exuberant, and brusque, while Kenedy, who had been a Quaker schoolteacher, was quiet, devout, and almost retiring in manner. Yet the association

14

of this rough-and-ready Irishman with the prim Kenedy was a lasting one. No doubt each sensed the loyalty and ability that the other had in abundance. Few if any altercations arose between them during the many years of their partnership.

For a while, however, friendship was all they had in common. They met only occasionally when their boats happened to put into the same port. Then one day Kenedy was asked by the American government to operate a steamboat on the Río Grande. The Mexican War had erupted, and experienced riverboat captains were needed. Kenedy told his superiors about his friend and wrote to King asking him to join him on that southern river. In May, 1847, Richard King went to South Texas for the first time, and he was never to leave it again for long. King landed at Boca del Río which was scarcely a town but rather a few weathered shacks perched on the dunes on the north side of the Río Grande near the mouth of the river.

North and east of Boca del Río was the land that was to become King's home. It was a no man's land, called "contentious" by Tom Lea. On many maps of the day it was marked simply "Desert" or "Wild Horse Desert," and its boundaries were the Nueces River on the north and the Río Grande on the south. In fact, it was this very land, butted against the Gulf of Mexico, which had been a principal cause of the war with Mexico. The area was populated, but not by "Christians," as R. B. Cunninghame Graham liked to term Europeans. It did have a goodly supply of other life, which included the unusual, such as armadillos, javelinas, and *paisanos* (roadrunners); the beautiful, such as white-tailed deer, quail, and turkeys; and the treacherous, such as the Karankawa Indians. Also present were the mustangs and the longhorns, which could be included in any of the three groups, depending on one's experience.

Tom Lea has characterized the Karankawa Indians as "seven-foot cannibals, rubbed in alligator oil, who had for centuries murderously disputed the passage of all men."[1] Texas claimed the land (a claim Mexico denied), but the Karankawas had it.

On the day Richard King arrived at Boca del Río, General Winfield Scott was well on his way toward winning the war in Mexico City, and Taylor

[1] Tom Lea, *The King Ranch*, I, 12.

15

was enjoying life in Monterrey. Logistics is never easy in war. The men of an army must eat; they need clothes; they wear out equipment. Yet none are employed in production, and everything must be supplied. King and his friend Kenedy were soon busy hauling up and down and across the river at the will and pleasure of the United States Army.

By 1847, when hostilities ceased, King and Kenedy had become important leaders in a bold land that needed men with vision and determination. They were such men as that "contentious" country called for, and they in turn, having looked around them well, liked what they saw. One thing was sure: river transportation had a future. They were soon paddling up and down the river in steamboats of their own design, accumulating capital for further ventures.

For King, new ventures were not long in coming. In 1852 he decided to attend a fair in Corpus Christi and with a few companions set out northeastward on horseback. He was fascinated by the countryside. As the group neared Corpus Christi, traveling along Santa Gertrudis Creek, they came to a beautiful spot. There was water—in fact, the first fresh water they had encountered (except for occasional brackish ponds and streams) since leaving the Arroyo Colorado, which they had crossed soon after leaving Brownsville. The sight of the clear, cool waters of Santa Gertrudis Creek must have been refreshing to King and the other parched riders, and the cool spring that added its water to the creek at the spot must have made the scene enticing. One can picture the tall, dark horseman dismounting, lying down, and putting his dusty face into the water to drink, little realizing that before many years had passed he would be the master of the land for many leagues around him.

This general area, which had once been the site of the Rancho de Santa Gertrudis, was rich in tall, strong, green grass. Texas wildflowers, so colorful in April, were evident in a bewildering variety of hues, with deep-tone colors of blue, purple, and red. Here and there appeared a patch of purest gold. Colors were splashed around like paint on a canvas by Monet. All of this, mind you, in an area that appeared on the maps of the time as desert and was referred to by Mexicans on both sides of the Río Grande as El Desierto de los Muertos, the Desert of the Dead.

16

Although the region struck Captain King as a garden, it had not been an Eden for earlier occupants. For them it had been a dark and bloody ground, and it would again be stained with human blood before the tall stranger held his title securely. An earlier "owner" had erred in stretching out the hand of friendship to some passing Indians. A knife in the bowels had released his grip.

The wildlife had not changed in the interval. Deer and mustangs could be seen in the distance, and birds chattered in the mesquite. Although there were patches of thick brush, or *brasada*, much of the country was still open. Prairie fires set by the Indians kept it that way. There was an abundance of curly mesquite grass and the matchless aromatic *huajillo*, both excellent food for grazing animals. There was also prickly pear, growing as tall as a man on horseback, and the *tasajillo*, with its innumerable thorns and its brilliant red berries that have always been irresistible to quail and turkeys.[2]

The occasional drought was hard on the live-oak stands, but it never seemed to bother the mesquite.[3] Perhaps it even produced a heavier bean crop later in the summer. Then there was the ever-present huisache, and the coma, with its dirklike thorns and its blue berries. According to local tradition, it is because of the coma plant that the white-winged dove coos, calling, "*Comer comas, comer comas.*"

These are some of the sights that Captain King doubtless observed as he jogged along the old wagon road, whose ruts had been dug by General Zachary Taylor and his army in 1846. The army, attracted by the site, had camped near the original Santa Gertrudis Rancho. Its beauty was a natural attraction then as it is today.

The Mexicans had long since abandoned the region. In 1839, General José María Cavalizo had ordered all the Mexicans between the Nueces and the Río Grande to pack up and leave. The settlers had had time to gather only

2 For a thorough description of this fabulous country, see J. Frank Dobie, *A Vaquero of the Brush Country*, 202–203.

3 Curious though it may seem, the mesquite was spread primarily by the horses, who loved mesquite beans and searched for them. As soon as the bean pods ripened, the horses were out looking for them. When the pods fall naturally, they seldom germinate. When they are picked up by a horse and pass through his digestive tract, the heat and fluids soften the beans so that they germinate when they are dropped. Surrounded as they are by fertilizer, the beans get a good start. Mesquite spreads rapidly in pastures where horses are kept.

17

a few of their cattle and horses, and those that remained had continued to increase. The land between the rivers then became a favorite hunting ground for bands of desperadoes, Mexican and American, looking for longhorns and mustangs. John Salmon Ford referred to encounters between these bands as "collisions."

So it was that in April, 1852, Captain Richard King first saw Santa Gertrudis Creek. It was a land that was to become as familiar to him as only a home can be. He had no idea when he set out for the fair in Corpus Christi that the land known as Wild Horse Desert would soon be his empire—that the steamboater would soon have a new home and the once abandoned Rancho de Santa Gertrudis a new master.

3. Starting the Santa Gertrudis

$\mathbf{B}$ACK on the river again, Captain King observed that steamboats had a habit of wearing out and falling apart. Looking north across the Río Grande, he recalled the beautiful spring at Santa Gertrudis and the flower-bedecked land around it. The rich grass would support a wealth of cattle and horses. Along the river he had talked with several Mexican families who had received grants of land from the Spanish and later Mexican governments. The grants lay north of the Río Grande, unoccupied, in a region now owned by the United States. The Indians and the outlaws had abandoned the area. The Mexicans did not think much of their holdings, even though their rights of title were valid, confirmed by the Texas legislature, which had acknowledged the ownership of land grants by rightful heirs and lawful purchasers.

Perhaps in the beginning Captain King planned to indulge in ranching only as a hobby. But, as Lea puts it: "King proved to be no absentee silent partner. Instead, he was absent more and more from the river, devoting himself to the nascent rancho. Its problems lured him. Its rough life pleased him. He took hold of it shortly after its inception."[1]

The man King chose to help him during his first ranching days was Gideon K. ("Legs") Lewis. King had met Lewis while steamboating on the Río Grande during the war. Lewis was an outstanding figure and, ac-

---

[1] Lea, *The King Ranch*, I, 102.

cording to Holland McCombs, a handsome, talented, swashbuckling rip of a charmer. He led a fabulous life, and Lady Luck seemed always ready to smile on him.

Lewis was born in Ohio, but his family moved to New Orleans while he was a child, and he grew up with the soft tongue and inherent gallantry of the southern gentleman. While still a young man, he enlisted in Captain H. W. Allen's Orleans Company for service in Texas during its fight for independence. There he found himself one of the members of the ill-fated Mier Expedition of 1842. With his usual luck, he was spared the fate of many of his comrades, who were shot by the Mexicans. He was taken to Perote Castle on a death march during which he earned his nickname, "Legs," because of his hardihood and seeming tirelessness. At the castle, as Walter P. Lane wrote in his memoirs, Lewis's "good looks materially assisted him, . . . as the Mexican ladies, who were very susceptible to manly beauty, gave him many a square meal."[2] After Lewis gained his freedom in 1844, he went to Galveston and became editor of the *Galveston News*. He was soon a great favorite of Mirabeau Buonaparte Lamar, onetime general in Houston's army and president of Texas.

When war broke out between the United States and Mexico, Legs Lewis could not stay home. He signed up, conducted himself gallantly, and came out of the war a captain of the Texas Rangers. When he was discharged, he went to Corpus Christi and again entered the newspaper business. For a partner he chose one of the best-known land promoters in South Texas, Colonel Henry Lawrence Kinney. It was Kinney who organized the fair that first took Richard King to Corpus Christi.

Lewis's familiarity with the Rancho de Santa Gertrudis led to his arrangement with Captain King. Both Lewis and Kinney knew about the Santa Gertrudis property, and they decided to find a capable person to settle on it. When King showed up in Corpus Christi, he seemed to have all the requirements. Perhaps Lewis suggested a partnership at the time, pointing out that the Santa Gertrudis, which had proved too great a challenge to all those who had tried to tame it, might be just their bowl of clabber. He may

---

2 "Adventures and Recollections of Walter P. Lane" (ed. by Louis P. Lane in 1887), quoted by Holland McCombs in King Ranch manuscript, Chapter. VI, 42.

also have pointed out that he could watch over the ranch when the captain was away on the river. In the end King joined forces with Lewis and bought the ranch. For a man looking forward to a home and children and a chance to stay with his family instead of constantly plying the river, a ranch beat the steamboat business a country mile.

According to Walter Prescott Webb, in *The Texas Rangers*, in August, 1852, General James S. Gillett mustered three companies of Rangers for service. Legs Lewis was placed in command of the company stationed at Corpus Christi shortly after he and King established their first cow camp on Santa Gertrudis Creek. Having a captain of the Texas Rangers as a partner was a real advantage, King realized, for the bitter struggle to tame the strip between the Nueces and the Río Grande had now begun in earnest. The new owners had no intention of hiding or running. Whatever was in store, they would meet it head on, and if a fight was indicated, so be it.

John S. Ford, an outstanding Ranger of his day, was unstinting in his praise of the two young men and of their courage in establishing headquarters for a new Rancho de Santa Gertrudis. In his "Memoirs" he wrote:

> In 1852 Capt. Richard King, in company with G. K. Lewis, better known as "Legs" Lewis, established a cattle ranch on the Santa Gertrudis Creek. They made their headquarters near where my old camp stood in 1849. This cattle camp became a stopping place for wayfarers, a sort of city of refuge for all classes, the timorous and the hungry. The men who held it were of no ordinary mould. They had gone to stay. It was no easy matter to scare them.[3]

On July 25, 1853, the purchase of the Santa Gertrudis was recorded in Starr County Courthouse in Río Grande City. All the existing heirs of the original owner, Juan Mendiola, set their hands and seals to a warranty deed conveying the Santa Gertrudis to Richard King for three hundred dol-

[3] John S. Ford, "Memoirs," V, 881. Ford was born in South Carolina on May 21, 1815. By the time he was sixteen, he was a schoolteacher—not because he was a genius but because he could read. He was attending medical school when he was infected by the urge to go to Texas. He soon became well known in his adopted land and was elected to the House of Representatives of the last congress of the Texas Republic. All his life he alternated between military service and newspaper editing, at both of which professions he was proficient. He wrote his "Memoirs," a fascinating account of day-to-day life in the Texas of the time.

lars. The sale was a windfall to the Mendiolas, for the land was worthless to them. With that sum Richard King bought title to about 15,550 acres of land at less than two cents an acre. Acquiring it proved much easier than ranching it, as the previous owners had discovered.

At first the King Ranch was just a simple cow camp located on one of the two small rises, the only ones for miles around. The little hill, scarcely a hundred feet high, ended in a bluff overlooking a nest of seep springs bordering Santa Gertrudis Creek. The land had few trees but a lot of grass. What trees there were—occasional mottes of mesquite, laurel, hackberry, and ebony—could be found along or near the shallow creek beds.

One of the problems facing the captain was the lack of year-round water. He had to gamble on rain, but he hedged his bet by building reservoirs. The biggest reservoir was the Tranquitas Dam, which was the only place between the Nueces and the Arroyo Colorado where a thousand head of horses or cattle could water all year long.

The original cow camp must have been a picturesque sight. It consisted of a group of dark-brown wattle adobe huts—*jacales*, as the Mexicans called them. The largest hut served as a commissary and stockade. The corrals were constructed of six-foot mesquite logs as straight as possible, laid horizontally and bound together between two upright mesquite posts. The ends were interwoven to make them sturdier.

In the beginning Captain King had few animals on the ranch, but what he had were varied. The captain was interested in acquiring and developing any livestock which could be raised profitably. From the outset King and Lewis were stockmen, not just cowmen. Everything they owned —cattle, horses, sheep, goats, and hogs—was raised to sell.

When a general drought came to the Río Grande country in 1854, soon after the ranch was established, King acted with typical sagacity. He had three priceless assets for that country: grass, the Tranquitas Dam, and money. He rode southwest across the Río Grande, looking for cattle at Mier and Camargo. He bought any livestock that looked able to walk—cattle, horses, goats, and sheep. It is said that King's purchases in 1854 brought a minor boom to the cow towns of Mier and Camargo. The Mexicans drove their stock to town from the parched ranges of the outlying ranchos, and,

22

as they said, "*El Capitan King, con dinero y sin miedo,*" bought and bought.

On one of his last purchasing trips King, in a master stroke, showed the breadth of vision for which he was to become famous—and thereby forestalled any future labor shortage on his ranch. At a small village south of Camargo he purchased all the available livestock. Then, realizing that the villagers were left with nothing, he asked all of them to return with him to the Rancho de Santa Gertrudis. After much conversation, and seeing no real alternative, the Mexicans agreed.

The motley procession—men, women, children, dogs, cats, chickens, pigs, mules, oxen, guineas, pet javelinas, parrots, monkeys—wended its way to Camargo, crossed the Río Grande, and trudged northeast toward the ranch. One can picture the hundred or so people, young and old, tall and short, weak and strong, some walking, some riding the big two-wheeled *carretas,* some pushing wheelbarrows loaded with goods, some carrying their meager possessions. No doubt the dust of the drought-ridden country heralded the strange band's approach and marked its passage long after it had disappeared.

These families were to furnish the nucleus of the proud Kineños, as the Mexican *vaqueros* on the ranch came to be called. From the time the entourage arrived at the ranch, Santa Gertrudis was their home and their children's home and their children's children's home. Together with others who came later they formed as expert a set of horsemen and as loyal a group of employees as ever gathered on the grasslands of the United States.

Richard King selected Mexican cowboys by choice. He could have hired Irish settlers from the San Patricio region or English or German immigrants who had come to Texas in response to Kinney's land promotions. King chose to cast his lot with the Spanish Mexicans. He believed that they understood cattle and ranching; moreover, he liked them, understood them, and respected them. They returned his respect and responded to the opportunity he gave them.

Fittingly enough, the first cash income for the Santa Gertrudis was produced by the sale of horses and mules, about $23 worth, on June 19, 1854. A second sale took place on June 26, when the ranch sold $1,000 worth of mares to White and Gardner. Unfortunately, we have no description of those sales, and the reason for them is unknown. King subsequently sold many horses, but he was primarily interested in building up his cattle herds, not in selling. Horses were probably in great demand, especially if they had been "gentled" (which generally meant that they had been ridden once or twice). In September of the same year the ranch sold five mules and one horse for $280.

Captain King soon made it clear that he wanted the best possible ranch horses and that he intended to improve them. He bought the best horse stock available and sold only those he did not want. On August 3, 1854, he paid $250 for a gray American stallion, probably brought in from one of the southern states (American as used in this context means a horse from the United States to distinguish it from one purchased in Mexico). On the same day the ranch paid one William Wright $300 for a bay American stallion. On November 28, 1854, King purchased a sorrel stud named Whirlpool (certainly a typical Quarter Horse name) for $600. Before the year's end the ranch bought five more American horses for a total of $735 and one American mare for $135. King also bought a gelding for $100. He was paying prices that would buy the best horses in the country. A mustang broken to the saddle could be bought for $3.50 at that time. When one realizes that he had paid only $300 for the Santa Gertrudis Ranch, the value he placed on good horseflesh becomes obvious. He was well aware that his safety and that of his men would often depend on the fleetness of his horses. The purchases also demonstrate why from the start the King Ranch men have been famous for the quality of their mounts.

4. Recollections of an Old Kineño

ONE of the more colorful accounts of the beginnings of the King Ranch was recorded by an old Kineño named Víctor Rodríguez Alvarado, who spent his life as a King Ranch *vaquero*.[1] He remembered what he had seen and what his parents and grandparents had told him. This chapter is really his.

As Alvarado recalled it, Captain King bought his first cows and a red roan bull from two brothers, Pedro and Anselmo Flores, who lived in Tamaulipas, Mexico. From the same ranch he bought a remuda of horses. News that a Texan was buying livestock soon got around, and many people brought horses and cattle to sell to the captain. King bought twenty-five or thirty mares and a stallion in addition to those he had already purchased. Alvarado explained that he was sure of the numbers because the cowboy who drove the horses and cattle to the Santa Gertrudis for Captain King was his grandmother's brother, Damón Ortiz.

When Captain King built his first ranch headquarters in 1854, he obtained the services of Alvarado's grandfather, Francisco Alvarado, who had built many houses. At the time Francisco was working at the Rincón de la Boveda Ranch, about a dozen miles south of the Santa Gertrudis. When he went to work for King, his son and his grandson, Víctor, accompanied him

---

[1] Víctor Rodríguez Alvarado dictated his "Memoirs" in Cotulla, Texas, in August, 1937. The information in this chapter was taken from a photostatic copy of the "Memoirs."

to help with the building. The houses were constructed of rough mesquite wood, and the holes and cracks were filled with dirt. The roofs were thatched. When the houses were completed, corrals were built of the plentiful mesquite wood. The workmen dug a hole for a water tank and bedded it with tough *sacahuiste* grass. They loaded the dirt from the hole onto a dry cowhide, tied their lariats to the hide, climbed on their horses, and dragged the dirt away.

Alvarado's memories then moved ahead more than ten years. After the Civil War ended, he recalled, Captain King put out two or three camps of about ten cowboys each to rope and brand the wild cattle that were roaming the area. There were a chuck wagon, a cook, and about twenty-five horses at each camp. The men branded all the wild cattle they could find, putting King's brand on them. The boss of the work was Santiago (James) Richardson.

After King had stocked his ranch with cattle, he decided to build a packing house to process his beef. When this venture proved impractical, he decided to drive the cattle to St. Louis. A thousand steers were rounded up and, with William Brai as the boss, driven overland to St. Louis, where King, who had accompanied the drive, sold them for a good price. King also sold all the horses and equipment and put the boys aboard a boat bound for Corpus Christi. With the proceeds of the sale he bought more land, the Agua Dulce, west of Corpus Christi. While in St. Louis, he bought his first slick wire, and he put his brother-in-law, Hiram Chamberlain, to work fencing the six square miles of Agua Dulce.

As Alvarado recalled, there was one large pasture fenced with boards that held a great many wild cattle. King had left them there for many years, and cattle of all ages could be found in the pasture, all dangerous to work, since they had never been around people. All of the land was covered with brush. There were at that time four outfits, each with ten *vaqueros*, a boss, a cook, and a remuda man. It took five weeks to round up that pastureful of cattle, and a great herd was assembled. Some of the cattle, the most elusive and dangerous of all, had escaped the roundup. To drive them out of the brush two camps were selected, one bossed by Will Doughty and the other by Will's son, Mac.

All the remaining cattle had to be roped, for they would not drive.

Most of them were bulls. It was fortunate that the ranch had good cow horses, but even so, many horses were lost. Finally *vaquero* Juan Pérez was hooked by a bull which he had roped and from which he was trying to free his rope. Alvarado said: "That was when we needed to work with a cape, so we could defend ourselves. Every day after work was over, we would cut out a bull, cut his horns, and put him in a round corral. Then, one by one, with a canvas sack for a cape, we would go in with him and learn to dodge and work the bull with the canvas." Even when they finished that roundup, there were a few smart cattle left. Those the *vaqueros* hunted with guns, just like deer, and killed them for meat.

After the cattle were cleared from the pasture, the horses were next. According to Alvarado, the two best horsemen were Luís Robles and Julian Cantú, and they were put in charge of bringing in the *mesteños*. Some proved hard to catch. Since Robert J. Kleberg, Sr., who was now running the ranch, wanted the pasture cleared for other purposes, he let it be known that anyone who wanted to catch *mesteños* could keep all he captured. Many men responded. They built pens and trapped the horses until all of them were gone.

Alvarado remembered another incident involving Luís Robles. The horseman had a habit of drinking too much. He was a great rider, but when he had been drinking he could not stay on his horse. It would buck when he tried to mount. One night after a drinking session in Corpus Christi, Robles got on his horse three times and three times was thrown off. He became so enraged that he pulled out his pistol and shot the horse. Officers immediately arrested him and put him in jail. His wife realized that his situation could be serious, since many lawmen were not overly considerate of the Mexican Americans. She spoke to Kleberg, who went to Corpus Christi and saw that Robles was freed. As Alvarado said, Kleberg always stood by his men when they were in trouble.

27

5. The Captain Takes a Wife

Iт was while he was a steamboat operator on the Río Grande that Richard King met Henrietta Maria Morse Chamberlain. Henrietta was the daughter of a newly arrived Presbyterian minister who had answered a call to tend a flock in the border town of Brownsville. The good reverend was unable to find a home and had to rent a houseboat. He tied up his new home where Richard King always docked his riverboat when he came to town. When the captain arrived and found his usual docking area already taken, he blasted the occupants of the houseboat in precise, explicit, and profane terms. The only person who heard him turned out to be an attractive seventeen-year-old girl, who withered the captain with a few choice though lady-like words, to the embarrassment of the captain and the obvious enjoyment of his crew. The captain had met his match.

The courtship of the rough sailor may have been somewhat subdued before the refinement of the eastern-schooled girl, but it was determined. He was circumspect—though not shy, for the latter characteristic was lacking in the captain. He even attended his first prayer meeting, after prevailing on Mifflin Kenedy to introduce him to the young lady. King began to arrange his business so that he could tie up in Brownsville more often. The captain's suit was not to be denied, and Henrietta ultimately fell in love with him. It took the ranch-owning riverman about four years to convince her father that he was worthy of her hand, but he persevered, and on December 9, 1854,

28

Budd H. Fry, the deputy county clerk of Cameron County, issued a license to "join in the bonds of matrimony Miss Henrietta Chamberlain and Captain Richard King."[1]

In attendance at one particular evening service of the First Presbyterian Church of Brownsville were two nervous individuals, Henrietta and Richard, who were to be married after the service. The bride, sitting with the choir, wore a new gown of peach-colored ruffled silk with a bodice of white silk mull. The hymns, prayers, and sermon may have seemed unduly long to the prospective groom, dressed in unaccustomed finery and stiff new boots. Finally the service ended, and the marriage ceremony began. Henrietta came down from the choir, and the captain stepped up to the front. Standing in front of the altar, the Reverend Mr. Chamberlain solemnly united his daughter and Richard King in the bonds of holy matrimony.

On the following day the minister went to the courthouse and recorded the following: "This certifies that the parties named in the preceding license were duly married by the undersigned, an ordained Minister of the Gospel, in the First Presbyterian Church of this city, on the evening of the 10th of December, 1854."[2]

For their honeymoon the newlyweds went to the Santa Gertrudis Ranch, where the captain was beginning to carve out a home and an empire. For the journey he had purchased a special coach, fitted with curtains and other trappings essential to a lady. The trip from Brownsville took four days. Armed men escorted the carriage, and a cook accompanied the party to prepare the meals. Evenings spent by the glowing coals of a campfire must have been most enjoyable. In Tom Lea's words: "Blurred shapes of oak mottes and dim thickets of thorns stood upon a night horizon of prairies in starlight, and coyotes sang. Camps moved early: horses snorted in the chill at the first gray light, and harness rings clinked when the travelers took the jolting road again."[3]

Sixty years later Mrs. King wrote her memories of that honeymoon, expressing doubt that it had ever fallen to the lot of any other bride to have

[1] Marriage records, Cameron County, Texas, A, 387.
[2] *Ibid.*
[3] Lea, *The King Ranch,* I, 128.

had as happy a honeymoon. On horseback she and the captain roamed the broad prairies of the ranch. When they tired, they took a siesta under the shade of a mesquite tree. When she went to the ranch as a bride, the small ranch house was little more than a *jacal*. Her kitchen was so small that larger utensils had to be hung on the wall outside the house. Their favorite food in those days was roast venison (whether the captain was saving beef or whether they simply preferred venison she did not say).

When the new ranch house was completed and they were settled, Mrs. King became hostess to all travelers who came their way. The doors of the Santa Gertrudis were always open to wayfarers. She was the ministering angel to the ranch employees, who revered her almost from the day she arrived. Accustomed to missionary work, she continued it without breaking stride, answering the needs of every Kineño. To them she was La Madama and La Patrona. She was unfailingly kind, considerate, and sympathetic.

Since she had never entered into the social life of Brownsville, she never missed it. She was happy in a life devoted to her husband, to the children born to them, and to the ranch folk, smoothing their troubles, responding to their needs. Except for brief vacations, such as a well-remembered vacation in Kentucky, where she accompanied the captain on a horse-buying trip, that was her life from the day the honeymoon coach arrived at the little cow camp on the banks of Santa Gertrudis Creek.

6. Kineños

WHEN Captain King purchased the livestock belonging to the people of the little Mexican village south of Camargo and moved the families to the Nueces strip, he assured the ranch the nucleus of the labor force necessary to operate a large cattle spread. A successful ranch must have trained, loyal hands—and all the good ones do. When a man with Captain King's vision comes along, whose ambitions and goals are on a grandiose scale, loyal, capable men are doubly important, since the very size of the venture makes constant personal supervision impractical.

The first-generation *vaqueros* proved trustworthy and loyal, and whenever additional hands were needed, King hired more Mexicans. His ranch foremen were generally Anglo-Americans, but most cow camps were bossed by Kineños. When he hired a new hand, one of the first things the captain did was find out how much money the man owed and to whom. He then paid off the man's debts. The realistic captain was aware that an honest man (the only kind he wanted) has a sense of responsibility to one who has trusted him with money. By paying off the debt, King transferred that loyalty and trust to himself.

The Kineño was expected to work hard for the ranch. He could not work for anyone else, not even part time. But the Kineño knew that if he did his part he received something of great value—security for himself and his family. A secure future was not common in the strip of land between Nueces

31

and the Río Grande in the 1800's. The captain (and his heirs after him) never guaranteed anything. He never had to. His actions spoke for him louder than words. The Kineños only had to look around. They could see that the hands who were faithful to the ranch while they were young and active were taken care of when they became ill or disabled and when they grew old. A home and necessities were provided as long as they were needed.

The children raised on the ranch generally wanted to follow in their fathers' footsteps and to remain on the land that was their home. Most of them wanted to work with horses and cattle, but other occupations were open to them. For those with the necessary skills there were forges to be heated, plates to be filled with food, sheep to be herded, hogs to be butchered, horses to be broken, houses to be built, brush to be cleared, and a hundred other tasks. Some occupations were quite specialized, such as making the famous King Ranch saddle blankets, woven from the *cafe con leche* colored wool that was grown, sheared, carded, and spun on the ranch—as it still is today.

The origins of the King Ranch saddle blanket lie in an incident that occurred about fifty years ago. One day Bob Kleberg was joking with some Kineños, telling them that the saddle blankets the ranch bought for the *vaqueros* were not really as good as some of the ones the old-timers had woven in Mexico. He claimed that the people on the ranch could not weave blankets. The next day one of the Kineños came to Kleberg and said that there was a man in grubbers' camp who could weave a saddle blanket if Kleberg would tell him the size he wanted. In due course Bob Kleberg was presented with a beautiful saddle blanket. He immediately told the blanket maker that he need not clear any more land—that the ranch would build him a house where he could spend his time weaving blankets for the ranch. That Kineño and his family have been weaving blankets ever since.[1]

A curious bond arose between the Kineño and the *patrón* in those dangerous early years, when they depended on each other for their lives. A feeling of mutual responsibility and trust arose that still clings. The Kineño rode not only for the *patrón* but with the *patrón*. There is a difference. The

[1] This account was related to the author in a letter dated May 20, 1969, Denhardt Files, King Ranch Folder No. 1.

Kineños belonged to the Santa Gertrudis, and the Santa Gertrudis belonged to the *patrón*. When they fought off bandits and rustlers, they were fighting for their homes and jobs and for the homes and jobs of their fathers and their sons. The welfare of the ranch was the goal of both *patrón* and Kineño. Thus was born a loyalty too personal to buy.

No doubt, to many outsiders the ranch seemed like a feudal domain. The important difference was that it was not peopled by serfs. Every Kineño was free to draw his wages and ride out the gate any day he wished. Though many have done so through the years, those who elected to enter other fields have always had a special feeling for their early years on the ranch and have returned to visit their families and the ranch as often as possible.

On rare occasions bad apples turned up among the help in the early days. Sometimes they were renegades or spies sent in by someone with designs on King Ranch property. It is known, for example, that Juan Nepomuceno Cortina, whose rustling activities kept the border in turmoil for years, sent spies to work on the ranch. In most cases it did not take the Kineños long to find them out. Although ranch records do not say what happened to spies when they were discovered, there is little doubt that they were promptly deactivated.

Though Captain King was one of the first ranchers in the area, he was not the only one. In the 1850's and 1860's several cattlemen from the United States, as well as some of Mexican descent, established ranches near the border. All of the land north and east of the Río Grande had become part of the United States when the Treaty of Guadalupe Hidalgo was signed on February 2, 1848. Until that time the boundary between Texas and Mexico had been the Nueces River. One of the first acts of the Texas state legislature was to create four counties—Nueces, Cameron, Starr, and Webb—out of the newly acquired territory between the Nueces and the Río Grande. Nueces County, the home of the Santa Gertrudis, was the most isolated. The other three counties bordered the Río Grande, where the settlements were. According to the records, nine thousand people were living in the strip south of the Nueces River at the time. All but about five hundred of them lived along the north bank of the Río Grande, and most of them were Spanish Americans. Many still considered themselves Mexican citizens. In the second half of the nineteenth century, the formative period of the King Ranch, the strip was further divided into eight counties, and the population increased to fifty thousand persons, mostly Mexican.

It was a time of tension and conflict. Most of the Anglo-Texans appear to have been adventurers, determined to wrest the land from its Mexican owners, whom they treated as foreigners (Americans farther north treated the Indians the same way). The fact that Mexicans and Indians had lived on the land for hundreds of years had little weight with the newcomers; if they did not speak English, they were foreigners. Few Mexican landowners were able to keep their ranches together once the Anglo-Americans began to arrive in large numbers.

Fortunately, some of the newcomers, such as Captain King and Mifflin Kenedy, had a different view of the Spanish-speaking population. They treated the earlier settlers fairly, paying for all the land they acquired. In fact, they occasionally paid several times over for the same piece of land when new heirs appeared on the scene.

As the new ranches were established, the owners had to decide whether they wanted Anglos or Mexicans for ranch hands. The owner who, like Captain King, chose Spanish-speaking *vaqueros*, also acquired the role of *patrón*. The *patrón* system, as understood by the *vaqueros*, meant that the owner was much more than just a boss to cuss when his back was turned and to collect wages from once a month. To the Mexican ranch hand a *patrón* was a protector, a judge, and the last word in any dispute.

The *patrón* system was strengthened by the precarious position of the Mexican in South Texas. Raids by bandits and rustlers across the border into the Nueces strip made any solitary *vaquero* a suspect and one who as often as not was strung up to the nearest available mesquite or shot on the spot. Since his American captors probably spoke no Spanish, protestations of innocence were useless. Consequently, the safest range for the *vaquero* was on the ranch of his *patrón*, in company with his fellow workers. The *patrón* system that evolved along the Mexican border from Texas to California constituted a brief period of semifeudal life. The system was political and social as well as economic. Its existence was inevitable under the circumstances, and its benevolent characteristics have been maintained to this day on the King Ranch.

A rather curious phenomenon arose on these Latin-oriented Anglo-American estates. The new owners had to adjust themselves to the psychology, habits, and traditions of their *vaqueros*. Otherwise the enterprise would never have survived the first twenty years—let alone the five generations through which the King Ranch has prospered. During the first critical generation a new culture and a new tongue were but loosely plastered over the Anglo-American rancher, but this culture became an integral part of his children's lives. To a large degree the later generations were Latinized, and the "new culture" now represents a way of life for most of the old families south of San Antonio. Their food, clothes, speech, and even radio and television programs are fashioned to suit a culture that is neither "American" nor "Mexican" but "Spanish South Texan." Even the road signs are bilingual.

The loyalty of the Kineños to the King Ranch demonstrates the value of the system and helps explain why it has worked so well for so long. There have been too many outstanding Kineños to list them all, though their history is in a very real sense the history of the King Ranch. Some family names have been important down through the years, among them Quintanilla, Treviño, De Luna, García, Cantú, Longoría, Silva Montalbo, Alegria, and Mendietta. Although they do not say much, their quiet dignity illustrates their awareness of their accomplishments and their realization that they, and the land, are the bedrock from which the ranch has grown.

7. The Little Snake ᴠᴠ

THE trademark of a cattleman is his brand, and, like a trademark, it soon becomes a mark of distinction and the symbol of his reputation. The ᴠᴠ, or Running W, of the King Ranch is such a brand.

Perhaps a good story to illustrate the value of the Running W—or any good brand, for that matter—is one about the King Ranch trail boss, Walter Billingsley. One day, while trailing several thousand of Captain King's steers north to market, Billingsley found himself in need of money. Riding into a small Kansas town, he tried to cash a draft on the ranch. There were not, of course, any telephones, and the nearest telegraph was miles away at the railway line. The local banker, not knowing Billingsley, refused to honor the draft. The trail boss did not know anybody in the area, but he had an idea. He rode back to camp and told the boys to load up and drive the whole kit and caboodle down the main street of the town. He then returned to the bank, and as the herd went by, he pointed out the Running W on all the cattle, horses, mules, wagon, and other ranch equipment. The size of the herd, the excellence of the remuda, and the quality of the equipment spoke louder than words of the solvency of the owner and the worth of the brand. Billingsley got his money.

Strange as it may seem, the origin of the Running W, one of the most famous brands ever to grace the side of horse or cow, is unknown. Many people have claimed to know how it came into being. They can tell exactly

36

where, when, and by whom it was originated. The trouble is that they all tell different stories. Tom Lea, in his book on the history of the King Ranch, does not attempt to say for sure how it started.

The first horses and cattle branded by Captain King did not carry the Ꮚ𝒰. The captain used and recorded almost forty brands in his ranching operations. Some he inherited with horses or cattle or land he purchased; others he or his men devised.

Not surprisingly, many of his brands reveal Mexican or Spanish influence. The old Spanish brands were in many cases taken from the rubrics of the owners' signatures. Sometimes Aztec signs and symbols were worked into a brand. Such brands combined artistry, symbolism, and imagination, qualities generally lacking in brands of Anglo-Saxon origin. The average American cowman was too practical to want an intricate brand. When one looks through the old brand books in courthouses along the Río Grande, it is easy to pick out those of Spanish origin at a glance. The simple, straight letters, numbers, or bars so common in American brands are not found in most Latin marks. The Ꮚ𝒰, at first glance at least, appears to be a happy combination of the simplicity of the American brand and the flowing lines characteristic of the Spanish.

The first brand registered by Captain Richard King was one he designed himself, and it is typical of the man in that it honored his wife, Henrietta King. It was the HK Connected, or ⊬𝒦. Mrs. King was delighted. Years later she told her grandchildren how thrilled she was to ride out on the range with her husband and see the cattle branded with her initials. The HK Connected was registered by Reuben Holbein, clerk of Nueces County, in Corpus Christi on March 20, 1859. It was several months before the captain registered his own brand, although there is reason to believe that he had been using it for some time. This brand, which he also designed himself, was the Ere Flecha, or R Arrow, ⊬. The third brand he recorded was the LK Connected, or 𝒦. This brand was used on the cattle he and Legs Lewis, his first ranching partner, owned together. On June 27, 1859, Holbein registered these two brands in Nueces County. The fourth brand registered was similar to the third and was used to distinguish cattle owned jointly with James Walworth, another partner. This brand was the KL with a V added, 𝒦.

The famous Running W did not come into general use until Captain King and Mifflin Kenedy, his long-term partner in steamboating and ranching, decided to split up their holdings. When the livestock were divided, each had to adopt a new brand to distinguish his herds. As Tom Lea wrote:

> After seventeen eventful years of ranching in partnerships, Richard King became the sole owner of the Santa Gertrudis. According to the terms by which he and Kenedy divided the livestock of R. King & Co., a new brand was required of each partner for the counterbranding of the sorted herds. Mifflin Kenedy chose for his own mark the Laurel Leaf ⌐, befitting his Rancho Laureles. Richard King used as the sign and symbol of his new sole ownership a clean-cut, simple mark destined for enduring fame, the Running W.[1]

The early Kineños called the ᗩᐁᗡ brand Viborita, or Little Snake. Some said that it represented a caution sign, meaning "Cuidado," "Be careful, don't step on me." One old *vaquero* thought that he remembered hearing that the Viborita came to the Santa Gertrudis with the *entrada*, the cattle from Camargo. If the Running W brand did by chance go back to the original stock Captain King brought from Mexico, its origin may be the serpent so familiar in Aztec symbolism.

Another possible origin was suggested by the late John Ashton, of Texas A & M University. Over the years Captain King purchased many parcels of land and the cattle thereon. In so doing, he acquired the brand with the land and cattle. Among such brands were two used by William Mann which he purchased in 1862. One was M A N, and the other was the Running M. Ashton's theory was that King simply decided to use the latter brand upside down. This explanation is almost too neat. The captain's originality and his desire to employ a brand truly representative of the ranch itself make the Mexican origin seem more likely.

Perhaps the actual origin of the brand lies in the story Bob Kleberg tells:

> The story goes, and this is from my father, that he [King] picked a brand that was the hardest to change with a running iron. When a calf is held on the ground with one foot pulled back, the hide is necessarily

[1] Lea, *The King Ranch*, I, 256–57.

pushed together. When this is stamped with the running ⱱⱱ branding iron, and the calf is allowed to get up, the brand is an irregular W and gives the appearance of a W that was put on with a running iron.

This brand is very difficult to change. Any good inspector could detect the change if it were made with a running iron. This is essentially the true story of the brand.[2]

The ⱱⱱ was not recorded at the county seat until February 9, 1869. It seems pretty certain that it was in use before that date, however, and there are indications it may have been used even before December 20, 1866. King registered the ⱱⱱ in Cameron County in 1872, in Bell County in April, 1876, and in Bosque County in May, 1876.

2 Letter dated May 20, 1969, Denhardt Files, King Ranch Folder No. 3.

8. Growth

For a number of years after the ranch began operations, the captain found it difficult to make a profit. The best he could do was to sell small lots of cattle and horses, and he could make more from his horses. He was too far away from populated areas to make many beef sales.

According to Leroy Graf, by 1861, King owned around twenty thousand head of cattle and three thousand horses. The Civil War brought a demand for horses and mules. Beef would have sold well if he had had some means of getting it to the armies, but transportation difficulties made such sales impossible. Other markets were completely disrupted during the war.

The price of beef dropped to two dollars a head—if one could find a buyer. The only available markets were the local ones and an occasional contract to supply beef, horses, or mules to whatever Confederate forces might be in the area.

The weather was also difficult during the early 1860's. A long drought set in that did not break until 1865 (many people blamed the prolonged dry spell on the artillery duels carried on by the armies). Owing to the drought and lack of supervision, many cattle drifted south, looking for grass and water. During the winter of 1863–64, a series of northers drove many more cattle southward. According to some estimates, as many as two hundred thousand head of cattle moved into South Texas during that winter, which came to be known as the "Big Drift." Brands from as far north as the Colorado River were encountered.

The ranch did find markets for tallow and hides. Before the days of electricity and natural gas, "tallow dips" were the common form of illumination, and many of the King Ranch steers were turned into tallow for candles in rendering plants erected on the ranch.[1] Most of the tallow was packed in barrels and shipped east from Port Isabel or Corpus Christi, depending on which plant had processed it. The remains of one of these rendering plants are still visible on the banks of the Santa Gertrudis, a few miles above the present headquarters.

Occasionally an eastern buyer could be talked into purchasing hides for harness, saddles, shoes, and other articles. Hoofs and horns were sometimes purchased by glue manufacturers, and hair, especially horse hair, could be sold for plaster, haircloth, cushions, and buggy seats. In short, the ranch could sell almost anything except beef. After the hide, hair, hoofs, horns, and tallow were taken, the meat was often left to rot or to be eaten by the hogs.

After the war ended, Captain King and Mifflin Kenedy decided to split up their holdings. The details of this division, which was accomplished in 1867 and 1868, give us an idea of the size of their operations. In August, 1872, Mifflin Kenedy testified before the General Claims Commission at Brownsville that, as of August 20, 1866, R. King and Company had owned 84,000 head of cattle, 5,400 head of horses, 17,000 sheep, 500 hogs, and 4,000 goats.[2] With as much livestock as that, all that was needed for the ranch to prosper was a market.

King and Kenedy realized that their holdings were becoming too large and too involved for any possible settlement of their estates by their heirs. The account books kept by the ranch showed that in 1867 the partners had $32,807.94 in their horse account. At the same time the cattle account contained $21,657.56—further evidence of the importance of horses on the ranch. When the partnership was dissolved, each man drew $16,403.97 from the horse account and $10,828.73 from the cattle account.

1 Paul Wellman, *The Trampling Herd*, 56–57.
2 McCombs, King Ranch manuscript, Chap. XV, 2195.

41

Captain King had been buying land for himself even before the partnership was dissolved, and afterward he began to buy in earnest. The Spanish-speaking people in the area had a saying that in time the *patrón* would buy all of the land between the Nueces and the Río Grande. King did want a lot of land, and he bought plenty. His concept of good business lay in the economies possible in large-scale production. Certain modern agricultural practices have proved him correct.

It is only natural that a man who buys 600,000 acres of land is going to become something of a legend in his time. Many who lack such a man's resources and energy belittle his efforts, and King was called a "robber baron" on occasion. Nothing could have been further from the truth. His careful legality in the purchase of the additional sixty tracts of land, varying in size from 300 to about 30,000 acres, demonstrates the falseness of such accusations. To begin with, his lawyers made all his purchases. He took possession of land only when they assured him that he had the right to do so. As mentioned earlier, he often paid for the same tract of land several times over to satisfy heirs who claimed part ownership.

The land he was buying was a fantastic jumble of Spanish-Mexican land grants. There were no section lines or township numbers. To complicate matters, in the period from 1770 to 1835 grants had been issued on lands with conflicting claims overlapping earlier grants. Under Spanish law each heir had an undivided *derecho*, or right. The magnitude of the task of buying such land was illustrated by King's efforts to purchase the San Juan de Carricitos grant, which necessitated buying the *derechos* of sixty-five heirs holding or claiming rights to the one piece of land. A less determined and resourceful man could never have completed the job.

As the years passed, King slowly acquired more land and saw his livestock increase both in number and in quality. The first adequate marketing was at last made possible as the railroad extended west across Kansas. Abilene and Dodge City became well acquainted with Running W cattle, as the next chapter will illustrate.

By 1884, however, the bloom was off the cattle market. Too many cattle were being driven north. Yet in spite of less favorable prices, King was

42

still selling cattle, still putting herds on the trail north. He was also adding to ranch income by marketing wool from his sheep—and by selling horses.

King found his horse business profitable. The horses he sold were far better than others on the market at the time. Many years of buying superior stallions and careful culling had resulted in horses respected wherever cowmen gathered. Among King's unusual traits was a preference for bands of horses of one color. The King Ranch remudas and manadas were composed of bays, sorrels, blacks, and grays, all carefully grouped by color.

Tom Lea tells an interesting story about how the ranch acquired one of its gray horses:

> One evening at dusk a stranger rode to the Santa Gertrudis commissary and asked to spend the night. He was mounted on a beautiful iron gray stallion; he was hospitably asked to stay. Captain King himself came out to look at the gray horse. He told the stranger that the stallion was one of the finest animals he had ever seen. The gray stood sixteen hands—bigger than the horses the Captain bred. When King had finished walking around the horse admiringly, he told the stranger to make himself at home, to stay awhile. The stranger expressed his thanks and explained that he must leave early the next morning. The Captain came out to bid him fair journey and courteously sent a vaquero to put the stranger upon the San Antonio [to Brownsville] road. When the time came for the vaquero to turn back, the stranger said, "Get down. I want to change with you. Take this horse back to Captain King and tell him that Jesse James sent him a gift with his compliments." Whether the stranger was Jesse James or not, the horse was an admirable fact. The big, strong, fine-limbed offspring he sired and the descendants carrying the iron gray's stamp were known at the ranch as the "Jesse James horses."[3]

During the last decade of the nineteenth century, the ranch operations were pretty well channeled, and the most profitable department was the one

[3] Lea, *The King Ranch*, I, 361–62. In a letter to the author dated May 20, 1969, Bob Kleberg wrote that his father had told him that the stranger was headed for Brownsville and had just come from San Antonio. He added that the *vaquero* took the stranger to the nearest gate on the road, about ten miles from the ranch house.

specializing in the production of horses and mules. For almost a quarter of a century, roughly from 1885 to 1910, the King Ranch was one of the world's leading producers of horses and mules. Thousands were sold, the principal buyers being the armies of the United States and Mexico, police departments in the larger cities, the carriage trade, lawyers and doctors, and the centers that supplied the South with work animals for the cotton fields.

A word or two about Mifflin Kenedy. When he and Captain King divided up their ranching interests, they also decided to fence the properties that comprised their respective ranches. Both men believed in the efficient operation of the grass and water they owned, and such operation was not practical on the open range. Before long Kenedy had completed thirty miles of heavy posts and three-plank fencing across the peninsula which formed his Laureles Ranch. (Kenedy would sell the Laureles to a Scottish syndicate in 1882, and Mrs. King would purchase the ranch from the syndicate in 1906.)

When Kenedy and King were in the steamboat business, Kenedy married Petra Vela de Vidal, the daughter of a Mexican rancher who lived at Mier. The Kenedys first settled in Brownsville but later moved to Corpus Christi to be near their ranching interests.

In later years, when Captain King became ill, Mifflin Kenedy was ever ready to help his old friend and former partner. He often drove out to the Santa Gertrudis to visit with King. Kenedy had troubles of his own in those days. His beloved Petra Vela also became ill. His son, James, who ran the La Parra Ranch for him, died of typhoid fever. Still later, when Captain King was dying in San Antonio, Mifflin Kenedy, grieving for his wife, who had recently died, came immediately to sit at his friend's deathbed. In his will King had named Kenedy one of the three executors of his estate.

The house in Corpus Christi which Kenedy had built for his wife was next door to the one which Robert J. Kleberg, Sr., and his wife lived during the winters while their children were in school. Kenedy's office was also in Corpus Christi. Only two of his six children survived him: a daughter, Sarah, who married a Corpus Christi doctor named Spohn, and a son, John G. Kenedy, who with his wife and two children managed the 390,000-acre

44

Kenedy Ranch south of the Santa Gertrudis. John Kenedy and Bob Kleberg were friendly rivals in many affairs, including Quarter Horse racing.

Mifflin Kenedy died of a heart attack on March 14, 1895, ten years after the death of his partner, Richard King.

9. Trail Drives

Until 1865 stockyards and slaughterhouses in the United States were for the most part local enterprises. Their problem was that as towns grew and began to encircle them they were asked to move. In Chicago a group of speculators, in an effort to resolve the problem, purchased 640 acres of land and sold it to beef-processing concerns. The result was the Chicago Union Stockyards. It opened for business on Christmas Day, 1865. From that day forward the financial success of the King Ranch was assured.

One of the great leaders in the meat-packing industry was Gustavus Franklin Swift. Concerned that only about 40 per cent of the steers grown for market proved edible, he soon found uses for the other 60 per cent in valuable by-products. Another program he developed was one of processing the animals as close to the source as possible and shipping only the finished products. The meat prices dropped as the by-products were used, and as the price of beef went down, the demand for beef and beef products increased. As Paul Wellman says, to their delight the factory worker and the bank clerk suddenly found that they could afford to eat meat. The United States became a nation of beefeaters.

Several things that would ultimately affect the cattle industry were occurring in widely separated sections of the country. In the heavily populated areas of the North and East there was a scarcity of beef. In Texas there had been a tremendous increase in the numbers of cattle—during the Civil

46

War not enough able-bodied men had been available to gather the cattle, and no markets had been available in any case. Another factor that was to act as a catalyst was the railroad. The Kansas Pacific Railway was stretching from Kansas City, Missouri, through Abilene, and on to Denver. The Santa Fe was moving southwest through Wichita and Dodge City toward Santa Fe, New Mexico. Boxcars from the hungry cities were reaching ever closer to the grasslands and cattle of Texas.

Fortune had first smiled on Richard King when the cotton road stretching from the warring South to Mexico crossed his lands. Now Lady Luck was to be generous again. His vast reservoir of cattle would soon help provide a lusty young nation with the beef it wanted. Chicago, Kansas City, and St. Louis were building the stockyards, and King Ranch steers worth two to five dollars on the ranch would soon be bringing twenty to forty dollars at the railheads. The cattle industry of the Great Plains was born in South Texas, and when the cattle reached the railroad, the packing industry became big business.

Early in 1866, Captain King sent his first cattle north, in the charge of Thomas Beynon. From that day until the drives ended, King was one of the largest operators. Some sources claim that the largest cattle drives in history originated on the ranches of King and Kenedy.

In 1875, King sent 60,000 head of cattle north into Kansas. The following year he sent 30,000 head.[1] In 1884, Walter Billingsley reached Dodge City with 5,600 King Ranch steers, certainly one of the largest single herds ever trailed north. Dobie wrote that Captain King often sent herds numbering as many as 3,500 head, adding that the herd Billingsley took north in 1884 was the talk of the countryside. After studying all available figures and statements made by such authorities as G. W. Saunders, E. S. Osgood, E. E. Dale, Charles Goodnight, and others, Dobie concluded that, "considering such a stock and their increase, the estimates of 10,000,000 cattle and 1,000,000 horses for the drives that followed [after 1866] during the next quarter century seem conservative."[2]

Another indication of the numbers sent north by Captain King is found

---

[1] *Corpus Christi Caller,* April 6, 1930.
[2] J. Frank Dobie, *The Longhorns,* 85.

in a letter from Mifflin Kenedy to Stephen Powers, dated May 10, 1877: " . . . and go up Tuesday to see King . . . and he will then be able to give you the lay of the land. . . . he has on the road now a little short of 1,800 head of cattle, one herd of over one hundred head of mules, and one hundred mares."[3]

In October, 1953, Holland McCombs interviewed an old-timer named Jack Maltsberger, who was then living in Cotulla, Texas. Though ninety-three years old at the time McCombs talked with him, Maltsberger was still mentally alert. He described how, as a boy living near San Antonio, he had seen the trail herds heading north. He remembered especially the King Ranch herds. They were a pretty sight, he said, with the cattle and horses matched in colors. The horses were uniform and beautiful. There were sorrel horses with red cattle, black horses with black cattle, and bay horses with brown cattle.

In one herd trailed north in 1875 by John Fitch, there were 4,737 steers, all branded with the Running W. With the steers went 113 horses, 9 mules, 3 mares, and a colt, all branded with the Running W on the shoulder and a K on the jaw.

[3] McCombs, King Ranch manuscript, Chapter XV, 2257.

48

10. The Family Grows

As the years came and went, Captain King's family grew larger and larger. Today they number well over one hundred. The descendants who run the ranch are the Klebergs. They have been the dominant force since the death of Captain King. The Kleberg branch of the family has been paramount in maintaining and improving the ranch and in developing the King Ranch Quarter Horses. A brief survey of the family members is necessary to help keep them straight, for they figure prominently throughout the rest of the book.

Captain King and his wife had five children: Richard, Jr., Robert Lee, Alice Gertrudis, Ella, and Henrietta.

Robert Kleberg had his first contact with Captain King in the course of a lawsuit which went to court in Corpus Christi in 1881. Kleberg, the opposition lawyer, handled the case deftly and won it. Then and there King decided that Kleberg was too talented to work for someone else and hired him. The two men left Corpus Christi late that evening, bound for the Santa Gertrudis. When they reached the ranch early the next morning, the captain roused his nineteen-year-old daughter, Alice, to make them some coffee. The captain and his new lawyer sat down in the living room to talk and wait. Alice hurried to the brick kitchen, kindled the fire, and soon had a pot of coffee boiling on the stove. She took the coffee and a plate of cookies into the dining room and then called her father and their guest. Peeking through the crack in the dining-room door, she watched her father and the handsome stranger. Before long the two young people met, and later Alice was to tell her children that they promptly fell in love. The courtship was, however, in Tom Lea's words, "exceedingly proper and unhurried."[1]

The years of constant warfare against the rugged frontier gradually took their toll of the captain. To keep going, he resorted more and more often to whisky. By January, 1885, he realized that the end was near. No longer could he drive his body, and even whisky failed to provide stimulus. He was a sick man and knew it, but for some time he would not leave his beloved Santa Gertrudis to consult his doctor in San Antonio. Finally, too weak to resist the entreaties of his wife and children, he agreed to go. His last instructions before leaving the ranch were to continue buying land and never to part with a foot of the precious Santa Gertrudis.

The captain's party arrived at the Menger Hotel in San Antonio, which was expecting them and had a suite ready. Dr. Ferdinand Herff, King's doctor, was also waiting for him. The examination did not take long. The captain was suffering from cancer of the stomach. On April 2, 1885, King dictated his will. Robert Kleberg put it into proper legal form, and the captain signed it.

A few days later, Captain King, the man Lea described as the "lonesome, hungry, tough-willed, hard-muscled, runaway apprentice from Manhattan," closed his eyes for the last time. His iron will and boundless energy had transformed that "contentious land" between the Nueces and the Río Grande. No longer was it untenanted and uninhabitable. It had become a vital part of the American scene.

Shortly after the captain's death the widowed Mrs. King returned to the ranch and appointed Robert Kleberg its manager. The legal aspects of the will were doubtless easier for Kleberg to handle than the new duties he acquired as ranch manager. As best he could he had to fill the boots of a man who had left his prints from South Texas to Kansas. To make the picture even more serious, the great western cattle boom had collapsed, and cattle prices had plummeted.

But Robert Kleberg had also come from sturdy stock. His father was

1 Lea, *The King Ranch*, I, 360.

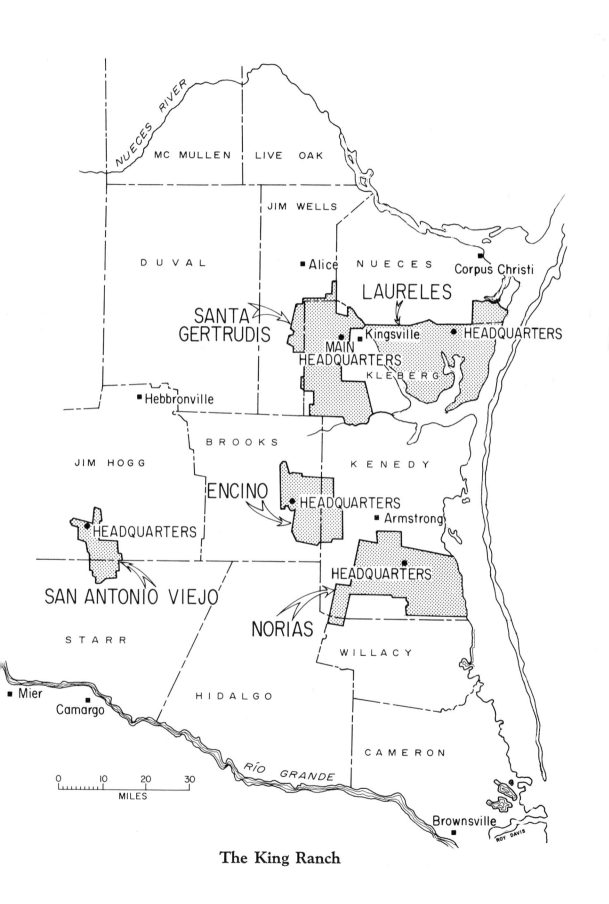

The King Ranch

born in Westphalia, Prussia, in 1803, and earned a degree in law from the University of Göttingen. The Prussian government of the day was a military dictatorship, and Kleberg's father, yearning to live in freedom, decided to go to America. He left Germany in 1834, and within a year he and his fellow immigrants were clearing land, building cabins, and farming near Harrisburg, Texas. In 1836 the advancing army of Santa Anna wiped them out. Kleberg joined Captain Mosely Baker's Texas Company and fought in the Texas War of Independence.

When the war was won, Kleberg and his wife settled at Cat Spring, in Austin County. Later they moved to a farm near Meyersville, in De Witt County. Four sons were born to them, Otto, Rudolph, Marcellus, and Robert. In 1837, Governor Sam Houston appointed Kleberg to the Texas Land Commission, and the following year Kleberg became chairman of the commission. A few years later Governor Lamar appointed him judge of Austin County. In 1846 he became county judge of De Witt County.

The judge's son Robert, Alice King's future husband, was born on the family farm near Meyersville in 1853. He was eight years old when the Civil War broke out. He watched two older brothers, Otto and Rudolph, ride off to fight for the South. After the war Robert attended the University of Virginia, from which he received a degree in law in 1880. He was admitted to the Texas bar when he was twenty-seven and joined the law firm of Stayton and Lackey in Cuero. A few months later he went to Corpus Christi to open a branch office of the firm. There he proudly hung up his shingle, "Stayton and Kleberg."

Captain King was doubtless acquainted with the Kleberg family before young Robert moved to Corpus Christi. There is reason to believe that King had met Robert's father, Judge Kleberg, who was well known throughout Texas both for his bravery during the Texas war and for his service in several important government positions. The captain was certainly acquainted with Robert's brother Marcellus, who was a state legislator. He also doubtless knew Rudolph Kleberg, whose law partner was an intimate of James B. Wells, the King Ranch lawyer. In short, the young man the captain brought home with him was not a total stranger.

In time Robert and Alice were married. They had five children: Richard

Mifflin, Robert Justus, Jr., Sarah, Alice, and Henrietta. Of the five, Richard, Robert, and Sarah would become active in ranch affairs. Richard married Mamie Searcy, and the couple had four children: Richard, Jr., Mary, Katherine, and Alice. Of the four, Richard, Jr., or Dick, as he is better known, has been most active and, as Bob Kleberg has grown older, has gradually taken over the day-to-day operations of the ranch.

Robert J. (Bob) Kleberg, Jr., married Helen Campbell. They had a daughter, Helen King. Bob Kleberg has been the driving force on the ranch during most of the twentieth century, taking over active management about the time of the outbreak of World War I. It is he who has been ultimately responsible for the Santa Gertrudis cattle, the famous King Ranch sorrel Quarter Horses, the King Ranch Thoroughbred racing stable, and, indeed, the welfare of the whole ranch. He has many talented and devoted assistants, but the final decisions on all important matters are his. Bob Kleberg is, in short, president of the King Ranch.

Sarah Kleberg, the oldest daughter of Robert, Sr., married twice. Her two capable sons, Robert Shelton and Belton Johnson, have a deep interest in the ranch. Sarah's sister Alice married Tom East, and together they set up their own ranching enterprise at Hebbronville, affiliated with the King Ranch. The youngest daughter of Robert, Sr., Henrietta, also married twice, to John Larkin and then to Thomas Armstrong. By her first husband she had four children, two sons and two daughters. One daughter, Ida Louise, married J. H. Clement, who is vice-president and secretary of the King Ranch. The other daughter, Henrietta, married John Armstrong, who is associated with the Big B Ranch operations of the King Ranch in Belle Glade, Florida.

These are the active members of the family today.

11. Key Personnel

To understand the history of the King Ranch Quarter Horses, it is necessary to know a little more about four particularly important members of the family. The first is, of course, Robert (Bob) Kleberg, Jr., president of the King Ranch. The other members of the quadrumvirate are Caesar Kleberg, Bob's cousin; Richard Mifflin Kleberg, Bob's older brother; and Richard Kleberg's son, Dick, presently chairman of the Board of Directors of the ranch and active manager whenever Bob is absent from the ranch.

Bob Kleberg was born on March 29, 1896, the fourth child of the Klebergs, and eight years younger than his older brother Richard. Bob always was a hard worker. The competence Bob achieved by hard work seemed to come without effort for Richard. Bob Kleberg's gifts of mind and body were as great or greater, but they needed more whetting. The younger man's mind (like his grin) was broader than Richard's, but it was not quite as spontaneous. They were alike in their love for the ranch, for horses and cow camps, and for all outdoor sports.

By the time Bob was seven, he was already working cattle with Caesar Kleberg and Sam Ragland. Ragland was a natural-born cattleman if there ever was one, and a good teacher as well. By the time young Bob was twelve, he could do anything any man on the ranch could do with a horse, a cow, or a gun. As he matured, he became proficient in hunting and shooting, in roping and cutting, and in the fine art of schooling a horse. He learned by doing, never content until he had mastered the work both in the cow camp and on the range.

When he was a child, Bob, with his father's blessing, lived with Ragland, the "old master." Sam, a bachelor, lived in a cottage about a hundred yards from the main house. During the many hours they spent together, in the cottage and on the range, the young man learned much from Sam, especially in the art of turning green grass into red beef.

Bob Kleberg never asked any more of life than to be a Texas cowman, although his responsibilities to the ranch eventually required him to become a geneticist, an oilman, a financier, and a regular visitor to distant cities and faraway lands. In time he associated with world leaders in industry, finance, agriculture, and government, but he always preferred the life of the ranchman and the association of the Kineños, to whom he returned as quickly as he could.

From childhood the diverse activities of the immense ranch fascinated Bob. His college education—for the most part self-designed—was endured only because it would help him further the success of the ranch. Early in 1916, while he was attending the University of Wisconsin School of Agriculture, he was summoned back to the ranch. His father was no longer a young man, and the ranch was shorthanded. From the day of his return, his life was filled with the various activities of the ranch. His main concern was to put all its operations on a solid financial basis. Yet somehow he also found the time to develop a new breed of American cattle, the Santa Gertrudis, and to perfect an outstanding strain of sorrel Quarter Horses. He also became one of the nation's most successful Thoroughbred breeders, developed new pasture grasses, and expanded the holdings and activities of the ranch into Kentucky, Pennsylvania, and Florida and ultimately into Argentina, Cuba, Brazil, Australia, Venezuela, and, at the latest account, Morocco.

Another Kleberg who exerted his influence on the development of the ranch horses was Caesar Kleberg. Caesar, Bob Kleberg's cousin, was the son of Bob's father's older brother, Rudolph. Casear's abilities soon became evident, and Mrs. King displayed a marked preference for the relative of her son-in-law. Caesar spent time in Washington as his father's congressional secretary. His ready wit and razor-sharp mind soon made him a favorite in the nation's capital. He was too much in love with Texas to stay long in Washington, however, and one day he appeared at the ranch. He was seldom to leave it again except for short business trips. He was employed by Mrs. King, since his uncle did not feel it proper to hire his own relatives.

Caesar's early life had been spent in cities, and, as Lea says, at the time of his arrival at the Santa Gertrudis his ignorance of ranching was extensive. An interesting story is told about one of his first contacts with ranch life. To test his adaptability to the ranch he was assigned to Sam Ragland, the best teacher available. Caesar's first trip with Sam was an early-morning buggy ride across some pasturelands. Once they were out in the wide-open spaces, Sam suddenly pulled up the team, tossed the reins to the young Caesar, and said, "Young fellow, watch the team." With that, he headed for some tall grass to tend to nature's call. Caesar held the reins a while. Then, remembering a newspaper in his pocket, he dropped the reins and pulled out the paper. The sudden movement and crackle of the paper made the horses bolt, right toward Ragland, who was hardly in a position for rapid movement. "Goddammit!" Ragland shouted. "You got a million acres here! Don't run over me!" Despite his tenderfoot background, Caesar learned quickly and soon became a key figure in ranch activities. To the Kleberg family he was more like an older and wiser brother than a cousin.

Caesar remained with the ranch until he died. He became a thoroughgoing cowman. He possessed keen insight about men, horses, and cattle. His consistently good advice led to his sobriquet, the Sage of Norias, as the ranch division he headed was called. He was one of Mrs. King's executors, together with Richard King III, Robert J. Kleberg, Sr., and James B. Wells.

A third key personality was the oldest of the children of Robert Kleberg, Sr., Richard Mifflin Kleberg. Richard was born in a rented two-story house in Corpus Christi on November 18, 1887. He was named after his grandfather Richard King and his grandfather's best friend, Mifflin Kenedy. As a child he showed great promise, and he lived to fulfill that promise in every respect. He was extremely competent and confident, both physically and intellectually. His contemporaries characterized him as engaging, articulate, lighthearted, gregarious, popular, and capable. In high school he was an outstanding student, the best baseball player, the best rider and roper, the

56

best sailor and hunter. He did everything with ease, grace, and aplomb. He had a photographic memory for details that interested him. He spoke Spanish as fluently as he spoke English. To the Spanish Americans he was *simpático*. He understood them, and they understood him.

His quick mind, ready tongue, and ability to mix with all people soon made it obvious that he could serve the ranch best in its public relations. When the occasion arose, he ran for Congress and served six terms. His principal work was naturally in the fields he loved most, agriculture and the outdoors. His two languages made him a natural for south-of-the-border missions. Richard spent thirteen years in public service in Washington. He then returned to Santa Gertrudis and to his first love, country life.

Dick Kleberg, the son of Richard M. Kleberg, Sr., has always been interested in the ranch and, since his return from college, active in its affairs. Born soon after Bob Kleberg started the Quarter Horse breeding program, today Dick is responsible for the continuation of the program, and he can take a keen personal pride in the continued excellence of the King Ranch Quarter Horses.

Dick Kleberg went to high school in Corpus Christi and attended Virginia Military Institute in 1934–35. From there he went to the University of Texas, from which he graduated in 1937. He then studied law for three years. In 1940 he married Mary Lewis Scott, and he and his wife have four children.

To all intents and purposes, Dick Kleberg is manager of the ranch, since Bob Kleberg is away much of the time, attending to operations in other states and countries. In 1968, when Mrs. Henrietta Armstrong, Bob Kleberg's sister, decided to give up active participation in ranch affairs, Dick became chairman of the board in her place.

These then are the men—Caesar, Richard, Dick, and, above all, Bob —who developed and made famous the King Ranch Quarter Horse. Others, such as Dr. J. K. Northway and Lauro Cavazos, also played important roles. Each will appear as the story unfolds.

PART II

12. The Quarter Horse Comes to Texas

THE Quarter Horse has been bred for a longer period of time than any other horse in America. Records of early Quarter Horses are found in colonial literature of the 1600's.[1] The Quarter Horse was developed to answer the need for quick breaking speed and levelheadedness (quiet disposition). His speed he obtained from imported English running stock. The English running horse is not referred to here as a Thoroughbred, because that breed was still a century or more away from entrance in a studbook. The quiet disposition and compact ruggedness of the Quarter Horse was inherited from Galloway stock from Scotland and from the Spanish blood already in America among the horses of the Indian tribes. The horses of the eastern Indians were descendants of Arab and Barb horses and were first obtained from Spanish settlements in Florida.

When the Quarter Horse lost quality or speed, the colonial breeder would infuse more English running blood. This admixture lengthened the horse's stride and improved his quality. When too much long-horse blood was introduced into the breed, the Quarter Horse lost his utilitarian characteristics of levelheadedness, compact conformation, and quick speed. In general, breeders belonged to two camps: those who believed in continuous infusions of English race-horse blood and those who for one reason or another

[1] For more information on colonial Quarter Horses, see Robert M. Denhardt, *Quarter Horses: A Story of Two Centuries,* 6–15.

refused to cross-breed with English racing stock. The most successful Quarter Horse breeders were those who cross-bred judiciously and maintained the characteristics which made their horses so valuable.

With the development of the Thoroughbred the long race became popular in the East. The Quarter Horse lost favor and followed the frontier westward. There he was everyman's utilitarian horse because he was such an easy keeper, so sensible, and so durable. When he finally reached the cow country of Texas in the 1800's, he found a permanent home.

It was in Texas that the Quarter Horse reached maturity and eventually became an official breed. The early breeders, some of whom will be discussed in the next chapter, carefully bred him for the qualities needed most in frontier ranching, which were still basically early speed and levelheadedness. From 1850 to 1940 very few Quarter Horse races were started from gates. Match racing was the favorite sport, and "lap-and-tap," "ask-and-answer" starts the rule. Under these conditions, levelheadedness was so important that breeding the Quarter Horse for short races never impaired his usefulness on the cattle ranch. If the Quarter Horse was too excitable, he could never be a successful race horse, any more than he could be a good cow horse.

In today's horse-racing scene, with organized races for several horses and compartmented gates to hold them still for the start, the quality of level-headedness is no longer of major importance to the race-horse breeder. Modern breeders, breeding for speed alone, must be careful or they will soon lose the other basic Quarter Horse characteristic, cow sense. Cow sense and a quiet disposition seem to go hand in hand. Lose one, and you lose the other. Lose them both, and you lose the Quarter Horse.

The early Texas breeders were interested in both speed and talent for cow work. For the most part it was a matter of emphasis among the breeders. Some put a premium on cow sense; others, on speed. But each kind of horse needed a good disposition, sure-footedness, and a low center of gravity. The last quality was manifested by a greater weight per hand than any other saddle breed. It also gave the Quarter Horse his unique conformation.

The horse program that was established on the King Ranch can be divided into three periods: the formative years under Captain King, the period when Robert J. Kleberg, Sr., guided ranch operations, and the period most important to this book, the era that has been dominated by Robert J. Kleberg, Jr.

While Captain King was alive, the main concern was to tame the wild grasslands between the Nueces and the Río Grande. To do so, good horses were essential, and the captain paid whatever price was necessary for the best. Consequently, the Santa Gertrudis early developed a reputation for good horses. The word good does not necessarily mean uniform, however. Blooded stock, some imported from as far away as Kentucky, built up the horse stock of the King Ranch until it became the best in the area. The program consisted simply of breeding the best available stallions to the ranch mares. These mares were Spanish-type range mares. No uniformity or special characteristics were demanded.

Robert J. Kleberg, Sr., who took over the ranch upon the death of the captain in 1885, generally continued the captain's breeding programs. He appears to have leaned toward a larger, harness-type animal because he found a better market for harness horses and mules. He also favored color uniformity. The stallions were turned out each spring into the immense pastures with their manadas of mares. Each stud selected a territory in the pasture and kept his mares together. Kleberg also tried to see that all the mares in each manada were of a similar type. Kleberg's tick-control program also indirectly helped the horse program. Every effort was made to clear the pastures of all non-essential breeding stock. Many inferior horses were rounded up and driven into Mexico.[2]

In 1916, Robert J. Kleberg, Jr., was summoned home from college to take over active supervision of the ranch. The ranch was a going concern by that time, but Bob was convinced that it had not yet reached its full potential. The grass was still not being turned into beef in the most efficient manner. To achieve that end he made it his business to find or to develop superior grass, superior cattle, and superior horses. He has never stopped searching

[2] It took many years to eliminate all the outlaw horses and cattle from the ranch. Tom Lea described the concerted efforts to capture the *cimarrones*. When an old hand named Stevens, who helped trap mustangs in the 1890's, was asked whether life on the ranch was civilized in those days, he replied, " 'Well, it didn't seem so wild and woolly to us then, but if anyone now had to go back to living like they did then, I reckon about half of us couldn't stand it.' " Lea, *The King Ranch*, II, 486–87.

63

for a grass that will put on more pounds, cattle that will mature more rapidly, and horses that can work more efficiently. His ultimate aim has been to assure that all forces on the ranch—the cattle, the horses, the land, and the climate—work as a team.

From the first, Bob Kleberg worked toward this goal with tremendous vitality, and the result of his dedication was to advance the interests of ranching throughout the world. New grasses were developed and old ones improved. The Santa Gertrudis cattle, a new American breed, were developed for the South Texas environment. No other American breed is hardier or more tick-resistant or carries a better beef carcass. The fact that the Santa Gertrudis were found to mature earlier and to weigh 15 to 20 per cent more than other breeds was just so much icing on the cake.

Another goal—the one that this book is concerned with—was a labor of love for Bob Kleberg, the improvement of ranch horses. Kleberg is a consummate horseman, and the selection and breeding of the sorrel King Ranch Quarter Horses has been one of the great pleasures of his life—one he began to enjoy almost from the day he became manager of the ranch.

Bob Kleberg was aware of the special characteristics of the Quarter Horse. He had ridden horses all his life, and he knew such Quarter Horse breeders as Ott Adams, George Clegg, and John Dial. He was not the only Texas rancher to discover that cow horses and the short-horse were kissin' cousins. When it became evident that the ranch horses left much to be desired as top cow horses, he naturally began looking for ways to improve them. The greatest difference between Kleberg and the other ranchers was that he decided to breed a strain that possessed the qualities he desired, not necessarily those that a purchaser would buy. He was successful in that goal. His ability to graft selected Thoroughbred features onto the Quarter Horse resulted in a new strain of sorrel Quarter Horses. Moreover, it turned out that what Bob Kleberg bred for the ranch also proved to be a most salable commodity. An examination of the horses he bred and the men who bred them will do much to explain the success of the King Ranch animals in the Quarter Horse world.

64

13. Early South Texas Horse Breeders

OR some reason South Texas has been blessed with more than its
share of great Quarter Horse breeders, and in one way or another all have had
influence on the development of the King Ranch horses. Starting in the
1850's with William Fleming, the list of breeders also includes such outstanding persons as W. W. Lock, Crawford Sykes, Joe Mangum, Dow and
Will Shely, Ott Adams, and George Clegg.[1]

William B. (Billy) Fleming was the founder of the famous Billy horse,
whose name is synonymous with the Quarter Horse of South Texas. This
area has in fact been called the "land of the Billys" after Fleming's famous
stallion.

Fleming was born in Georgia on November 18, 1830. As a young man
he was a Ranger on the Texas frontier, mainly engaged in fighting the Comanches (for the rest of his life he received a government pension for his frontier
services). He served four years in the Confederate Army and was wounded
many times. His right arm and hand were deformed as a result of those
wounds.

---

[1] For more information on early South Texas breeders see "Credit Given to Shelys," *Western
Livestock,* August, 1945; "George Clegg, Veteran Breeder of Top Quarter Horses," *Western Livestock Journal,* May, 1941; "The Billy Horse," *Western Livestock Journal,* May, 1941; "Traveler
Country," *Quarter Horse Journal,* December, 1954. Much of the material concerning the men in
this chapter was taken from the notes and clippings found in the Denhardt Files.

Fleming never married. He spent most of his life on his small ranch between Seguin and Gonzales. In his old age, when he was no longer able to take care of his beloved horses, he sold them to his friend Fred Matthies. Billy soon followed his horses to Matthies's home near Sequin and lived there until his death on April 30, 1911.

Fleming was a small, slender man with a mustache and a beard. His brand was the ace of clubs. He made his living breeding and selling horses and for a time was a partner of Tom King (no relation to the Kings of the Santa Gertrudis).

The horse Billy was Fleming's most famous stallion and was named for him. Billy was by Shiloh and out of Ram Cat by Steel Dust. Billy was the sire or grandsire of many famous horses, such as Pancho, Joe Collins, McCoy Billy, and Sykes Rondo. Billy is found high up in the pedigrees of Little Joe, King (Possum), Jim Ned, and both Joe Baileys.

After Billy, Rondo is probably the best-known South Texas horse. Tom Martin brought Rondo to Kyle, Texas, and sold him to Bill Lock. Rondo had been bred by Charles Haley, of Sweetwater, who lost him in a race at Fort Worth in 1885. Rondo was by Whalebone by Billy and out of Paisana by Brown Dick. When Lock bought Rondo from Martin, both Lock's and Rondo's fame was secure. From that time on Rondo was known as Lock's Rondo. There were several horses named Rondo, most of them descendants of the original Lock's Rondo.

W. W. (Bill) Lock raised and raced Quarter Horses at Kyle from 1887 to 1895. Nobody was raising faster horses, and Lock had difficulty matching his horses. As soon as other breeders saw his LO brand, they decided not to enter that particular race. Finally Lock decided to seek greener pastures. He moved north and settled in Greer County, Oklahoma, in 1895. He took Rondo and his other horses with him and continued racing and breeding Quarter Horses until his death in 1908. He kept his horses at Mangum, Oklahoma, where Rondo and Texas Chief made names for themselves. Rondo was responsible for many famous horses, such as Blue Jacket, Bonnie Bird, and Little Rondo. Little Rondo sired Waggoner's Yellow Jacket.

Joseph Marim Mangum and Crawford Sykes, both of Nixon, Texas, were partners in the horse business. Sykes's farm was about ten miles east

66

of Nixon, near Pandora. His brother, Columbus Sykes, who was also engaged in the horse business, lived at Stockdale. In 1876, Joe Mangum married Mattie Gillespie, who was related to Columbus Sykes, and the three breeders thus had close ties. Crawford Sykes's original horse stock was of Swagger and Billy Fleming breeding. Joe Mangum's principal contributions were some mares of Tiger blood, especially the well-known May Mangum.

The foundation stallion for the Sykes and Mangum horses was another Rondo, the horse known as Sykes Rondo, although the horse was actually bred by Joe Mangum. Sykes Rondo was by McCoy Billy by Billy, and his dam was a Tiger mare. One of the best Sykes- and Mangum-bred stallions, Blue Eyes, was sold to Dow and Will Shely, of Alfred, Texas.

The Shely brothers reached prominence as breeders somewhat later than Crawford Sykes, although they were contemporaries. The Shelys started breeding in the 1890's on the Palo Hueco Ranch, near Alfred. Will stayed on the farm, while Dow spent much of his time in San Antonio. They had a small but select group of Crockett mares and Blue Eyes, the stallion they bought from Sykes and Mangum. Blue Eyes had gained his first fame as a race horse and had established a world's record in Dallas that had stood for a number of years. He was sired by Sykes Rondo and out of May Mangum. The Shelys' second stallion was John Crowder, who was by Billy. They bred him to Blue Eyes' fillies, and the cross produced some of the fastest horses in Texas. Among the best known were Mamie Crowder and Lady S. Their third and best stallion was Traveler. During the years the Shelys owned Traveler, he sired such horses as Little Joe, Texas Chief, and King.

The Shelys finally dissolved their partnership and sold their ranch and horses. The two principal buyers at the horse sale were Ott Adams and Jack Hensen. Hensen took the horses he bought to North Texas, where some were later sold to Tom Burnett and the Waggoners.

Just as the Sykes and Mangum breeding farm owed much to William Fleming, and just as the Shelys gained from Sykes and Mangum, so too did Ott Adams obtain his basic stock from the Shelys. Somewhat later Bob Kleberg was to buy Little Joe mares from Ott Adams.

The first stallion Adams obtained from the Shelys was El Rey. Then he bought Little Joe, another Shely stud, from George Clegg. At the Shely

67

dispersion sale he bought Mamie Crowder, Julie Crowder, Moselle, and Little Kitty. Those six Shely horses were to establish Adams firmly as a top breeder of South Texas Billy horses.

Ott Adams was born in 1869 on a ranch in Llano County. As a young man he moved to South Texas, where he had heard the best horses were raised. He was a little man and looked like a jockey, though he never became one. He prided himself on raising fast horses, saying that they were the ones you could always sell. To do so, he bred speed to speed, and he would not buy or breed a horse that was not fast or from a fast family. Of all his stallions he liked Little Joe best. One of the few outside stallions used by Adams was Hickory Bill, sire of the King Ranch's Old Sorrel. Most of Adams's mares were of Rondo, John Crowder, or Peter McCue breeding. He considered Rondo the greatest horse he ever saw.

Ott Adams had a friendly rival in the short-horse game, George Clegg. George was born near Cuero, Texas, on April 2, 1872. His father was from Arkansas, and his mother was Irish. When he was in his early thirties, George moved to Alice and began breeding horses. Deciding that the two best lines of Quarter Horses were the Rondos and the Peter McCues, he accumulated some of each. His first purchase was a Rondo horse owned by Frank Wiley, of Cuero. Clegg named the horse Little Rondo. He purchased Little Joe as a colt from the Shelys, primarily for a racing horse, not to breed. Later he sold Little Joe to Ott Adams.

When Clegg heard that Mrs. Samuel Watkins, of Petersburg, Illinois, was selling her late husband's horses, he saw a chance to get some of the blood that had made Peter McCue so famous. He sent for several horses, including Hickory Bill, a son of Peter McCue, Lucretia M., and Hattie W. When George crossed Hickory Bill on his Rondo mares, he made his reputation as a breeder. His horses had a class and style often lacking in South Texas horses. They had sufficient speed and were good for racing, roping, or polo. Paul El and Sam Watkins are two well-known horses he bred, although no doubt his greatest was the Old Sorrel, who was bought as a colt by the King Ranch. George spent much of his later years helping in Bob Kleberg's Quarter Horse program. He died in Alice at the age of eighty-six.

One of George Clegg's great admirers was Colonel W. W. Sterling, of

68

Corpus Christi, a famous Texas Ranger. Sterling never tired of telling about the good Quarter Horses raised by his friend Clegg. One of Sterling's most interesting accounts of Clegg horses had to do with another friend of his, Sam Lane, who lived on the border. Lane bought a horse from Clegg and called him Little Rondo, after the horse's sire. He rode Little Rondo with just a strap around his neck. With this strap he would rope or cut cattle and do any other necessary work. This tale is a good illustration of the cow sense inherent in the Quarter Horse and also emphasizes his quiet, level disposition. There are not many stallions in other breeds that would tend to business under similar circumstances.

Lane's ranch, Guadalupe El Torero, was located in what is now Hidalgo County. The progeny of Little Rondo were much in demand on both sides of the Río Grande. One characteristic of Lane's horses, and one in which he took pride, was their endurance. Lane himself weighed well over two hundred pounds, and he and his equipment put right at three hundred pounds on the back of the horse he rode (which may well be one reason why he demanded endurance of his horses). He used to boast that he would not own a horse that couldn't carry him all day at a lope and bring him home that night.

Lane's pride in the ability of his Little Rondo horses involved him in a famous border incident of the early 1900's. It was a contest without rules or judges, and only nature's law of the survival of the fittest determined the outcome. Lane had a neighbor named Jesús Vela, who, incidentally, was a character in his own right. The two men could agree on the best whisky, the ideal woman, the nobility of the cowman, and the audacity of Teddy Roosevelt, but not on which was the best horseman or had the best horses.

One of their arguments about the relative endurance of their horses became so heated that they finally decided to settle the issue for all time. They hitched up one Lane horse and one Vela horse side by side to a buggy with wide metal tires of the type common in the sand country along the border. Both men climbed into the buggy. Since there were no roads or officials, distance and times were not recorded. However, Lane's horse, descended from Clegg's Little Rondo, was still on his feet pulling when Vela's horse fell dead in his tracks.

69

14. Dr. J. K. Northway

THE story of the formation of the special strain of King Ranch Quarter Horses is so complex that it is well-nigh impossible to present it in a neat chronological package. Many horses and many people are involved in the story. Some appear and disappear, and others enter the picture to stay. The next few chapters will be devoted to some of those individuals who have made a marked contribution to the King Ranch Quarter Horse.

The one individual other than Bob Kleberg who started on the ground floor with the breeding program and has been working with it constantly ever since is Dr. J. K. Northway, the internationally famous King Ranch veterinarian. For over fifty years he has worked on the ranch, and his association with Bob Kleberg has been more than just an employer-employee relationship. He has been both a friend and a counselor to Kleberg. No one can properly be called "adviser" to the head of the King Ranch. Kleberg is a good listener if a person has something to say that he finds important. He will ask questions of those he respects—although sometimes just to see whether they agree with him. He always carefully sifts the information he has and comes to his own independent conclusion. That is why the word counselor, rather than adviser, is used in speaking of Dr. Northway's relation to him.

Much of the time the day-to-day control of the breeding program has been in Dr. Northway's hands, although every key decision has been directed by, or cleared through, Bob Kleberg. Today, after half a century of close association, Dr. Northway can generally anticipate what Bob Kleberg wants done.

James Kellogg Northway was born in 1893 in San Antonio, Texas, where his father was a blacksmith. His earliest recollection of his mother is watching her riding a black stallion to the back steps of their home. She was riding side-saddle and holding his little brother on her lap. He recalls that "she extended me her hand so I could climb up behind."[1] As a boy he delivered the *San Antonio Express* on horseback to subscribers in his neighborhood. He is proud that he made his first dollar on a horse, and he hopes to make his last the same way.

As he was growing up, his interest in livestock, and especially horses, made him decide to be a veterinarian. He saved his money and eventually was able to attend one of the outstanding veterinary schools of the day, the Kansas City Veterinary College. While he was in Kansas City, he also met his future wife, Amber Gertrude Smith, whom he married the day before he graduated.

During his college years he spent summer vacations assisting a San Antonio veterinarian, and after graduation he continued to work with him. One day in 1916 the doctor told Northway that one of his best clients, Caesar Kleberg of the King Ranch, was having trouble and asked him to go to Kingsville. Northway made the trip, liked everything about the ranch and the people he met there, and decided then and there to make it his home.

So it was that Dr. J. K. Northway went to work for the King Ranch and moved his bride to Kingsville. In the early days Mrs. Northway found the small frontier town of Kingsville quite a change from Kansas City, but she and the doctor were very happy and soon made many friends in their new home in South Texas.

At first the Northways had trouble finding a permanent home. Bob Kleberg's father, Robert, Sr., soon resolved the problem. Kleberg drove into town almost every day, got off his horse a little way from his office, and

---

[1] Denhardt Files, King Ranch Tapes, reel No. 3. Much of the information in this and the following chapters was recorded on tape while the author was visiting the ranch during the summers of 1966–68.

walked down the Kingsville street greeting all his friends. One day Dr. Northway met Kleberg, who asked him how he liked Kingsville and his job. The
doctor said that he liked everything just fine but wished he had a place to
live. He explained to Kleberg that he had had to move three times in four
years. Kleberg said, "Go to the lumberyard [which the Klebergs owned] and
tell Mr. Gregg that you are to have one of those rent houses he just built.
I didn't want him to build that many anyway." Northway said, "Mr. Kleberg,
I don't have any money to buy a home with." Mr. Kleberg replied with a
grin, "Could you afford fifty dollars a month most months?"[2] Northway
lived in that house for quite a few years. When he moved the next time, it
was into a new home on the King Ranch built for him and Mrs. Northway on
the brow of a low hill overlooking the horse barns, north of the main house.

Dr. Northway admits to having four great interests in life: veterinary
medicine, horses, cattle, and land. He has been blessed with ample opportunity to indulge in all four. The ranch has thousands of head of livestock
of every description, and he has been able to practice as much veterinary
medicine as he desired. He is today acknowledged to be one of the two or
three leading veterinarians in the world. His name is indelibly linked with
the formation of a new breed of cattle—the Santa Gertrudis—and with a
new strain of horses—the sorrel Quarter Horses of the King Ranch. That
pretty well satisfies interests two and three. Living on one of the largest
pieces of privately owned real estate in the world and owning a nice ranch
of his own has fulfilled his fourth interest. That is why he says with conviction
that if he had his life to live over he would want to live it the same way.

During Dr. Northway's early years on the ranch, before oil was discovered in large quantities, everyone had to work hard. Bob Kleberg spent
a lot of time doing what he loved best, working cattle in the open. More
often than not the doctor was also there. Northway remembers one day in
the twenties when all the men were out working cattle. They rode into camp
late that evening, where the cook had a supper of beans, tortillas, and fresh
veal cooking over the open fire. A calf had broken its leg that day and had
been sent to the cook. After supper the men lay around the fire talking. Bob
Kleberg said, "Lauro, now don't answer too fast. Think a minute. How

2 Denhardt Files, King Ranch Tapes, reel No. 2.

72

much does it cost to run this camp?" Lauro Cavazos, the Santa Gertrudis foreman, pondered for a minute and then said, "Counting wear and tear on saddles and men, about seventy-five hundred dollars a year." Kleberg turned to Dr. Northway and asked how much a good colt would bring. "Five hundred dollars," answered Northway.[3] Then Bob asked Lauro and Doc to find enough colts to sell to keep the camp operating. Cash was not always easy to obtain in those days. There were some lean years, for all of the wealth of the ranch was in land and cattle. Kleberg would not sell any land, and there was not always a market for beef.

Dr. Northway says that when Caesar Kleberg took over the Norias Division of the ranch there were a lot of unbranded cattle on the division. One of Caesar's first moves was to put up some fences and brand the cattle. He sent out the Kineños to work from north to south, branding as they moved from camp to camp.

One day when the hands were near a water hole, who should come down to drink but a zebra dun mare with a black stripe down her back and black bars on her legs, accenting the canvas-gold of her body. She was a beautiful sight, and following her were three offspring, a baby, a yearling, and a two-year-old, all duns like their dam. It was concluded that, since there were no other stallions around, the oldest had sired the younger two. Caesar roped the two-year-old and used him as a stud. He called him the Wiley Sego Dun, after the cowman who first saw the group coming to water. Even today the name Wiley Sego Dun can be found in the pedigrees of some of the ranch horses.

Race meets were fairly common in those days, especially match races. The doctor recalls a scheduled match race that never came off. The race was to be run by Carrie Nation and Karnes City Jim. Jim was being handled by some gamblers. Carrie Nation's backers put her on the train in San Antonio, where she was stabled at the time, and shipped her to Kenedy. When she arrived and both sides had looked over the horses, the betting grew hotter and hotter and the tension higher and higher. Someone was going to be severely hurt no matter which side won.

The situation finally became so tense that the starter and the judges

3 Denhardt Files, King Ranch Tapes, reel No. 1.

found reasons why they could not perform their duties. The few others present who were trusted by both sides would not consider serving as substitutes. The sheriff was getting quite worried, for he knew that everything in town but the railroad station and the bank had been wagered on the outcome of the race. With his three armed deputies at his back he "persuaded" Carrie Nation's owners to load her quietly onto the boxcar standing on the siding. The brakes were released, and with a pinch bar the car was gently eased to the main track, where it was hitched to the San Antonio train. The sheriff heaved a deep sigh of relief as he watched the train, Carrie Nation, and her owners disappear down the track toward San Antonio.

Every year after the cotton harvest there were impromptu races in the Kingsville-Alice area. Each year a man named John Morgan took a Quarter Horse and a wagon and camped out. According to Dr. Northway, Morgan would tie the horse to the back of his wagon and match all the races he could. He would eventually return home with his wagon loaded with everything from sacks of grain to chickens and goats. One of his horses that gained some fame was Bueno Amigo, by One Tenth and out of Plain Jane by Little Joe.

At one time or another since his arrival at the ranch in 1916, Dr. Northway has come in contact with almost all the men and horses that developed the King Ranch Quarter Horses. First and foremost was Bob Kleberg, whom Northway has characterized as follows: "You tell him how something should be, and if he agrees with you he will say so, and then he will go down the center of the road with you and never look back." The doctor was also thinking of Bob Kleberg when he told me, "I like a man that will stand tied."[4]

The doctor claims that Caesar Kleberg was one of the best judges of horses in that family of experts. It was Caesar who brought the Old Sorrel to the ranch.[5] Dr. Northway remembers a comment that Bob Kleberg made to him after the horse was broken: "We are going on with this horse, and someday we will have saddle horses to be proud of, and you will have something to sell."

---

4 Denhardt Files, King Ranch Tapes, reel No. 1. The rest of the material in this chapter attributed to Dr. Northway occurs in either reel No. 1 or reel No. 2.

5 For the story of how Kleberg came to purchase the Old Sorrel, see Chapter 19.

If the doctor were to make a list of the expert horsemen he has known, he would include Will Shely, George Clegg, and Ott Adams, with Bob Kleberg right up there at the top. He would also place John Dial, of Goliad, Texas, high on the list. John Dial once made a comment that tickled the doctor. He said, "I don't know anything about horses, but they sure as hell can run." Another favorite saying of Dial's was, "If it's free, you better not take too much." Dial raised and raced Thoroughbreds as well as Quarter Horses. It was he who bought Chicaro in New Orleans and brought him to Texas. Some of Bob Kleberg's best Quarter Horses and Thoroughbreds can be traced to blood he obtained from Dial.

Dick Kleberg said that the first time he met John Dial was in Dr. Northway's office. The meeting took place years ago, and Kleberg's original impression of the man has always stayed with him. According to Dick, Dial was a small man. That day he was carrying a little black satchel. The doctor asked him if he could spend the night. John allowed as how he could. He opened his black bag, and Dick saw in it a bootjack, a clean shirt, and a bottle of whisky. He was "forted" and ready.

Bob Kleberg tells about the time Dial took a horse named Nobody's Friend to Mexico for a race. It was a big match with a lot of money up on each side. Dial's horse ran straight and true and won by three lengths on the pull. According to Kleberg:

> John Dial's horse won easily. He was standing alongside the general [the judge of the race] and said to the general that his horse won the race. The general said, "I am very sorry, Mr. Dial, but just as the horses came to the finish line I dropped my pencil. In stooping to pick it up, I missed the finish. We can either go up to the house and have a chicken dinner or run the race over." John Dial said he accepted the chicken dinner.[6]

The King Ranch owned a black horse by Boojum out of Pal, which was also named Nobody's Friend for Dial's original horse of that name.

John Dial, who will appear again in Chapter 15, probably helped Bob Kleberg as much as anybody to get good Quarter Horse mares. Among those

6 Letter from R. J. Kleberg, Jr., to Robert M. Denhardt, dated May 20, 1969, Denhardt Files, King Ranch Folder No. 3.

Dial obtained for Bob Kleberg or suggested that Bob buy were Ada Jones by Little Joe, Lady of the Lake by Little Joe, Plain Jane by Little Joe, Big Liz by Paul El, Ann Wilson by Jack Hare Jr., Johnny's Bay by Paul El, and Old Queen by Ace of Hearts. That group of mares helped build the framework for speed in the King Ranch horses.

To that select list Northway feels a few others should be added as among the best of the foundation outcross mares. His additions are Water Lilly by Yellow Jacket, High Gear by Magician, Pal by Alamo, and La Tachita by Naughty Boy III. Doc feels that one of the best nicks the ranch had was the Old Sorrel on Little Joe and Hickory Bill mares. Even today, he says, if this blood is diluted too much, the quality, performance, and uniformity demanded by the ranch are lost.

Although some of the original mares used in the Quarter Horse bands were of Quarter Horse origin, the breeding program outlined by Bob Kleberg called for controlled infusion of Thoroughbred blood. That goal was generally achieved by breeding Thoroughbred mares to ranch Quarter Horse stallions. The fillies that resulted were broken, and if they proved satisfactory, they were returned to the Quarter mare band. In that fashion over the years the blood of Bold Venture, Chicaro, Lovely Manners, Assault, Naughty Boy II, Remolino, and others found its way into the Quarter Horse manadas.[7]

According to Dr. Northway, most of the original fifty mares given to the Old Sorrel were already living on the ranch and carried a predominance of Thoroughbred blood. What they had in common was their ability to work cattle. They were proven cow horses. They were bays, browns, blacks, and sorrels. If any one bloodline was most prominent, it was the blood of the Lazarus mares, which will be discussed later. Most of the first colt crop was sorrel, and Bob Kleberg decided to try to concentrate the color as far as was consistent with performance.

Bob Kleberg obtained two of his best foundation mares, Lady of the Lake and Johnny's Bay, from John Armstrong, a short-horse man from who laid the chunk. The mares were obtained when Armstrong went to work and live on the ranch. He was working for Alonzo Taylor, of Hebbronville, when Kleberg offered him a job at sixty dollars a month plus room and board.

7 See Appendix, list 1.

76

John said that the offer sure sounded good but that he had two mares he just could not leave. Bob told Armstrong that he could keep them in his front yard if he wanted to. Eventually, in the 1930's, the ranch bought both mares for two hundred dollars each.

Dr. Northway once asked Johnny how fast his favorite mare, Lady of the Lake, could run. Armstrong answered that he didn't really know but that she had always been fast enough to win. When asked if he ever worried about a race, Johnny said, "No, not once the race was matched." One time before he went to work for the ranch, Armstrong matched Lady of the Lake with Hickory Switch, a half brother of the Old Sorrel. Hickory Switch was owned by a man named Ramón. Ramón would gamble on anything—horses, dice, chickens, or the date of the next rain. Johnny said that once the race was matched Ramón and his friends kept coming back with more money that they wanted covered. When the race was over and Hickory Switch had lost, Johnny just told them to put the money on his bed. When he went to his room after cooling off the mare, the mattress was covered six inches deep with nickels, dimes, quarters, and paper money.

Dr. Northway first saw Ernest Lane, who was later to gain fame running Miss Princess and other King Ranch horses, in 1916. Lane was buying mesquite wood from the ranch and freighting it to Odem, where he sold it for a dollar a cord. The doctor says that he can still see Ernest, who was a stalwart youth, putting his shoulder to the wagon wheel to help the mule get the wagon across Santa Gertrudis Creek.

Dr. Northway points out that from the beginning no new blood has been put into the King Ranch Quarter Horses except by indirect outcross. For example, the dams of Hired Hand, My Man, and El Shelton were all indirect outcrosses. Whenever the ranch personnel find a mare that they consider outstanding in every respect, they buy her and put her in the mare band. All her horse colts are gelded and ridden. Fillies are broken and used by the Kineños to determine whether they can work with cattle. If so, they are returned to the mare band and from then on are considered King Ranch Quarter mares.

Some of Dr. Northway's theories about the aims of the ranch breeding program and its success are of special interest. He has seen the King Ranch

Quarter Horses contribute to the uniformity of the Quarter Horse breed. This is due in large fashion to the Old Sorrel, who Northway says is the Eclipse of the Quarter Horse breed.

The doctor points out that, except for the King Ranch, in the early days of the Quarter Horse registry few breeders were able to concentrate their program solely on the production of superior cow horses. Most breeders lacked the necessary number of individuals or were diffuse in their aims. They did not know whether they should breed for the heavy-set bulldog type or the half-breed type. Many breeders changed their emphasis with the market. The King Ranch set out to produce a utility cow horse and has never deviated from that primary purpose. Thus the ranch was able to concentrate on the best blood to set the characteristics and to infuse the quality lacking in the haphazardly bred Quarter Horses of the early 1940's. The low withers, short necks, and straight shoulders found on many bulldog Quarter Horses were never permitted in King Ranch horses. To avoid those characteristics Bob Kleberg carefully infused Thoroughbred blood through outcross mares. The early speed of the Quarter Horse was also retained.

A few ranches tried to follow the King Ranch lead, but most fell along the way because of inadequate resources or because of the heavy demand for their best individuals. If they did not have a great stallion like Zantanon or the Old Sorrel and if they were unwilling to concentrate steadily on the good qualities in spite of changing public desires or financial demands, they did not produce a prepotent strain, as Bob Kleberg was able to do with the progeny of the Old Sorrel.

The ranch has always bred its Quarter Horses for cow work. Some other breeders have raised and are raising Quarter Horses to race. Kleberg races Thoroughbreds. The ranch is not adding more Thoroughbred blood because the Thoroughbred does not have the temperament that the ranch demands in its cow horses.

The Klebergs' criteria for a King Ranch cow horse are not complex. They want a cow horse to ride into the herd with his head up and his eyes and ears working. They want him able to break fast to turn a cow and then go back into a walk. As Dr. Northway says, a King Ranch Quarter Horse works cattle as a partner, not as a slave. The men do not want to have to tell

78

the horse every move to make and then dig him with a spur to see that he acts. They want a horse that the rider feels safe on when he ropes an animal. They want one that will not go to pieces in a bind. They do not like to see a horse wringing his tail or biting at the girth, at the man, or, for that matter, at the cows. A top horse on the King Ranch has been likened to an artist—he has a natural love for the work and a bred-in excellence in execution. The horse works with his rider just as a good bird dog works with a hunter. That is the way they are raising them. A horse that has to be directed in every step is like a bird dog that heels when you want him to hunt.

Dr. Northway sums it up simply by saying that on the King Ranch a good cow horse is one that works with you. If you have to work him, he is not a cow horse. Any properly bred and trained Quarter Horse will do so. The Thoroughbred, regardless of bloodlines, cannot. Even a beautifully trained Thoroughbred whose guidance is not particularly noticeable is nevertheless being worked by his rider. Get on the back of a good Quarter Horse and ride into the herd, and you can tell the difference.

These are the observations Dr. Northway made in summing up what the men of the King Ranch want to breed into their horses.

15. John Almond and Other Contributing Neighbors

JOHN Almond is a typical South Texan, except that he is more capable than most both as a rider and as a judge of horseflesh. Perhaps some of this know-how was bred into him by his horse-conscious family, which contains some of the best-known short-horse breeders in the country. Most of the information that follows was recorded during a pleasant day I spent with Almond talking about the King Ranch and Quarter Horses. Some of his recollections varied from the generally accepted reports, but it is difficult to question his facts since he was present at most of the events.

John's grandfather went to Texas from England in the middle 1800's and settled in Corpus Christi. He worked hard, saved his money, and soon owned a lumberyard. As he made money, he bought land. Before long he owned 2,377 acres. While he was selling lumber, he watched for especially good boards and put them away for the home he was planning to build. John says that in the house his grandfather finally built there were boards of many different widths and thicknesses, but nary a knot. The house is still standing, and it is just as solid as the day it was finished almost a hundred years ago.

When John's father was sixteen, his grandfather died, leaving one other son besides John's father and two daughters. The younger daughter, Josie, married Will Shely, the famous Quarter Horse breeder, who was raising horses on a farm near Alfred. John's father and Will Shely were thus brothers-in-law and close friends. In fact, John's Aunt Josie met Will when John's father brought Will home with him one evening.

Traveler did much for the Shelys, just as Traveler's son Little Joe was to do much for Ott Adams. Dow Shely had been watching Traveler for some time and had decided to buy him when he became available. The occasion came at the track in San Antonio in 1903. Shely paid Traveler's owner, Jack Cunningham, of Comanche, four hundred dollars for the aging stallion. Dow and Will Shely bred Traveler until the horse died in 1910.

John Almond grew up with horses—South Texas Quarter Horses for the most part. He learned much from his father and from his uncle, Will Shely. Although John was interested in racing, his real love was roping and raising good roping horses. He always kept a stallion or two and a few mares. When I first met John in the early 1900's, he had a son of Chicaro Bill and some really top mares.

John did a lot of roping and won considerable money on a Chicaro Bill gelding. He was a big horse, standing over fifteen hands and weighing at least twelve hundred pounds. The gelding's dam, one of the best mares John owned, was by Joe Abb, a stallion who also appears in the pedigree of several King Ranch horses. John bought the mare when Dr. Strickland was on his death bed. The doctor wanted to sell three horses: the mare, Joe Abb, and a brown horse. They were running loose in Antonio Pérez's pasture. Strickland offered all three to Almond for three hundred dollars. John was interested only in the mare and Joe Abb. The brown horse's neck came out too high to suit John. The last laugh was on him, John admits. Strickland gave the brown horse to Pérez, who let Arturo Gómez train him. The brown made a real running horse. They called him Little Henry. When he grew up, he had crooked legs, big feet, and a plain head, but he could fairly fly. His looks made him easy to match because he didn't look like a race horse.

Joe Abb went through several hands after Almond bought him in 1935. In a series of sales he was owned by Tom East, Alonzo Taylor, R. C. Tatum, O. W. Cardwell, and E. A. Showers. Showers registered him in 1941. He was sometimes referred to as the Strickland horse.

John Almond kept the mare by Joe Abb. Her first foal was sired by Zantanon, and John sold him to Bill Warren, first president of the American Quarter Horse Association. Bill called the good-looking sorrel colt Cucuracha. He was one of the first horses registered by the Quarter Horse Association. The mare's next foal was sired by Jiggs. Jiggs, a good stallion, was sired by Uncle Jimmy Gray. The colt Almond got out of his mare and Jiggs won ribbons at the horse shows in Beeville and at Kingsville. Almond then sold the colt to Tip Westfall, of Edna. The Strickland mare's next colt was Almond's roping gelding, who was sired by Chicaro Bill.

In 1938, John sold the Joe Abb mare to Bob Kleberg. She was never named, but merely referred to as the Strickland mare. Her dam was by the Sutherland horse who was by Hickory Bill. At the same time John sold another mare to Kleberg. This mare was a four-year-old by Chicaro Bill and out of a Billy Sunday mare Almond had bought from Jim Adams, Ott's brother. He sold her for one thousand dollars, an exceptionally good price for a brood mare at that time.

Chicaro Bill was by the Thoroughbred Chicaro and out of Verna Grace (Fair Chance) by Little Joe. His second dam was by Johnny Wilkins. Chicaro Bill was bred by John Dial, who raced him in California and then eventually sold him to L. T. Burns. Afterward Ronald Mason and Elmer Hepler owned Chicaro Bill briefly. Glen Chipperfield acquired him in 1943 or 1944 and registered him with the AQHA.

John Dial, of Goliad, was an outstanding horseman and breeder and a friend of John Almond. As a young man Dial was in the livery-stable business. In his spare time he was courting two girls, and he had a hard time deciding which one to marry. Neither girl's family was entirely happy with John's attentions. He finally made his choice, only to find that he could not get her parents' consent. One night the couple eloped, took shelter with John's friend George Clegg, and were married the next day. Eventually they received her family's blessing.

John Dial always liked fast horses, and he and Clegg had a long-standing, though friendly, feud when it came to horses and horsemanship. Once, according to Almond, John and George made a big wager on who was riding the faster horse. They took off after a steer, and both threw at the same time

The Old Sorrel

The Old Sorrel, the foundation stallion of all the King Ranch Quarter Horses.
It is to him that all the horses in the program trace their top lines on both sides
of their pedigree charts. The Old Sorrel was foaled in 1915 and was sired by
Hickory Bill and out of a Dr. Rose mare. This picture was taken shortly before
his death in 1945.

Hired Hand

Hired Hand, one of the last sons of the Old Sorrel, and the greatest. He was foaled in 1943 and out of Water Lilly. He is gradually replacing the Old Sorrel on the pedigree charts as the one individual to which all program animals must trace on their top lines. He was shown in halter and performance classes for several years by Loyd Jinkens with great success. He is shown here in 1955, when he was twelve years old.

Hired Hand

Hired Hand shown with Dr. J. K. Northway in 1968.

Charro

Charro, foaled in 1933, was by the Old Sorrel and out of Toalla, who was by the Thoroughbred Martins Best. Charro was used as a stallion by the King Ranch for five years and was then sold to the Remount Service of the Peruvian army.

Peppy

Peppy (top, young; bottom, mature), considered by many to be the greatest of the early-day Quarter Horses. He was foaled in 1934 and was by Little Richard and out of a daughter of Cardenal. No other horse was as widely shown and as universally recognized, and no other horse did as much to popularize the breed.

Babe Grande

Babe Grande, foaled in 1928, sired by the Old Sorrel and out of a Hickory Bill mare. Babe Grande was a natural-born cow horse, and he transmitted that quality to his offspring. So valuable was he for that purpose that he was used in the stud from 1931 to 1951.

Wimpy P-1

Wimpy, foaled in 1936, sired by Solis and out of Panda. Wimpy was a superb stallion, and because he placed first in the 1941 Fort Worth Stock Show he was given registration number 1 by the American Quarter Horse Association. To many he typified the ideal American Quarter Horse.

Macanudo

Macanudo, foaled in 1934, sired by the Old Sorrel and out of Canales Bell. Macanudo probably looked more like his sire than any other son of the Old Sorrel. Except for Babe Grande, Macanudo was the best cow horse of the first generation.

Ranchero

Ranchero, foaled in 1933, sired by Solis and out of Borega, who was by the Old Sorrel. He was one of the first of the second-generation stallions to be used in the stud.

Hired Hand's Cardinal

Hired Hand's Cardinal, foaled in 1949, was by Hired Hand and out of Listona Azule, who was by Peppy. His excellence in the stud helped convince the King Ranch that Hired Hand should take the place of the Old Sorrel. This picture was taken in 1955.

Hired Hand II

Hired Hand II, foaled in 1948, was sired by Hired Hand and out of La Perdita.
He is considered by some to be the best of the second-generation colts. This picture was taken in 1955.

Wimpy, Peppy, Macanudo, and Babe Grande

Four great stallions: Left to right, Wimpy, Peppy, Macanudo, and Babe Grande. All these horses were foaled before the American Quarter Horse Association was organized, and they did more than their share in assisting the new registry in its bid for public acceptance. They also firmly established the King Ranch as a premier breeder of Quarter Horses.

Catarina

Catarina, foaled in 1932, was sired by the Old Sorrel and out of a mare of Lazarus breeding. Catarina was one of the greatest show mares and performing individuals that the King Ranch raised. She was stolen from her pasture in the early 1940's and was never recovered, though a large reward was offered for information concerning her whereabouts.

Water Lilly

Water Lilly, foaled in 1920, is carried in the registry as sired by Yellow Jacket and out of a Waggoner mare. Water Lilly was one of the most valuable mares ever purchased by the King Ranch and placed in the breeding program. She was the dam of Lady Speck, Little Man, and the Old Sorrel's greatest son, Hired Hand. Any one of those three offspring would have made her famous.

Ada Jones

Ada Jones, foaled in 1918, was one of the greatest daughters of Little Joe. Her dam was Mamie Crowder. She was bred by Ott Adams. She was a great race mare in her day, and later was sold to Robert J. Kleberg, Jr., by John Dial. Among her progeny were Chicaro's Hallie, John Dial, and Cambiada. She died in 1941.

Lady of the Lake

Lady of the Lake, foaled in 1926, was one of the few mares sired by Little Joe that were gray. Her dam was Silver Queen. She was bred by Ott Adams and was raced successfully by Johnny Armstrong, who sold her to the King Ranch.

and both roped him at the same time, one around the neck, the other by a hind leg. All bets were off. They were always nip and tuck, first one winning and then the other.

John Almond says that John Dial would go down to Ott Adams's with a can of lard and a side of bacon and talk Ott out of almost any horse he owned. Somehow or another Ott always seemed to be in need of bacon and lard. That was how John got Lady of the Lake, Plain Jane, and Big Liz from Adams. Alonzo Taylor and Johnny Armstrong wound up with Lady of the Lake and Plain Jane. Big Liz went to a man named Groll, a Dutchman living in Berclair, in Goliad County. Groll bred Big Liz to Chicaro Bill and got a running mare, Jenny Lee. He kept one of her fillies and bred her to Top Deck and got Glory Be Good, a hell of a race horse, according to John Almond. Groll later traded Big Liz to Tom Burns. Eventually all these mares wound up on the King Ranch as part of the Quarter Horse program.

John Almond said the first time he ever saw John Dial was at Ott Adams's. Dial was there with some lard and bacon. Ott had a little Quarter Horse he was especially proud of, and John says that he was a dandy. Ott led out the colt to show him to Dial and said, "Now what do you think of him, John?" John walked around him slowly and then said, "Well, Ott, I'll tell you. If he were mine, I would take him way back up into Tony Pérez's pasture. Then I'd cut him and roll him under the fence and never breathe a word of it to anyone."[1] Almond was a young man then and didn't know the two men very well. He was sure he was going to see a fight. Almond says there never was a pair like Dial and Adams around horses.

As mentioned above, Big Liz was sold to Tom Burns. She had a suckling colt by Chicaro Bill and had been bred back to him. When Tom sold Big Liz to Bob Kleberg, he was to get the colt she was carrying. The mare died when the colt was about three months old, and Tom raised the colt. He paid a Mexican helper to pick up mesquite beans, which he ground and mixed with molasses. He fed this mixture to the colt, and Almond says that you should have seen that colt bloom. Ott Adams saw him and liked him so well that he bought him. He named him Solo Mio.

In earlier days there were a lot of races around Kingsville. Most of

[1] Denhardt Files, King Ranch Tapes, reel No. 4

83

them were held on the Old King Ranch track, which is now a housing project. Bob Kleberg would generally attend the races and would buy any outstanding Quarter mares that showed up. According to Almond, that is how he acquired some of his best mares, such as High Gear and Pal. High Gear was one of the best. She could do it all—work cattle, rope, and race.

John Almond said that the King Ranch had a name for buying the best mares and raising top horses. However, one never ran into many horses with a Running W on them at the race tracks or at the rodeos and ropings. Not many were for sale, and those that were the cowboys couldn't afford to buy. Even in the 1930's they were selling for $500, at a time when one could buy a broke horse and a good prospect for $125 elsewhere.

George Clegg was another breeder who was always in the market for a good mare, according to Almond. Any time he found a mare that could do something better than any of his mares, he bought her. That is, of course, the reason for his reputation as a top breeder. George also gave away a lot of good horses. Rodeo performer Ike Rude went to Alice almost every winter. He would admire one of George's good colts, and George would give it to him.

According to John Almond, not many of the better King Ranch horses were ever used outside the ranch. Some of the boys from the ranch would occasionally rope at nearby towns, such as Kingsville, Raymondville, and Falfurrias. He remembers one gray stud from the ranch. He was owned by Henry Timmerman and was out of Lady of the Lake. One roping contest, in 1936 or 1937, was held right in the middle of the Kingsville race track. Bob Kleberg furnished the cattle—all white Brahmans—and roped on High Gear.

John Almond especially remembers one race meet held at Kingsville. Kleberg had matched Nobody's Friend against a little horse of Ernest Lane's called Bumps. Nobody's Friend bucked out of the gate. He lost to Bumps but ran the race in twenty-three seconds. Kleberg then put Nobody's Friend back in the starting gate, alone that time, and he ran the quarter in twenty-two flat. He just had buck on his mind.

At the same meet was an old man named Dan Scrubbs, from Alice. He said to Almond, "You know, Bob ought to think more of his friends and quit running that horse." Sure enough, says John Almond, it wasn't long until Bob Kleberg gave Nobody's Friend to a Mexican general.

Nobody's Friend was the result of crossing Boojum, one of the fastest Thoroughbreds that ever lived, with the Quarter Mare Pal. He was the Champion Racing Quarter Horse stallion of the world in 1942 when he won both races for three-year-olds in Tucson, besting Gold Deer, Wonder Lad, and Domino. In the World's Championship Race that year he was beaten only by the great Shue Fly. She beat him by a nose in track record time. He was, however, erratic, to say the least. Pal was by Alamo, and it was from Alamo that Nobody's Friend got his desire to buck, not from Boojum.

Dick Kleberg also has a story about Nobody's Friend. He said that if his uncle ever named a horse right it was when he named Nobody's Friend. One year, probably 1941, Bob Kleberg asked Dick to go to the Eagle Pass race meet, since he could not attend himself. At the time George Clegg was running Nobody's Friend for the ranch. Ab Nichols, of Gilbert, Arizona, also attended the Eagle Pass meet. He owned a great old horse named Clabber, who could outrun anything except a race horse. They raced and roped on him, let him serve about a hundred mares a year, and turned him out in the pasture whenever he wasn't busy. On the same day he raced with Nobody's Friend he beat two other horses, Balmy L and Little Joe Jr., both pretty fair horses. When the day was over, he had beaten all three horses in exactly the same time, twenty-three seconds flat.

Ab Nichols or one of his friends persuaded George to run Nobody's Friend against Clabber. According to Dick Kleberg, Clabber beat the hell out of him. Kleberg continued: "George's room was next to mine at the hotel in Eagle Pass. About five A.M. I heard a knocking on the door. I thought it was mine and got up to answer it. There at the next door, which was George's room, were a couple of his friends bringing him a big bowl of clabber."[2]

John Almond and Ott Adams were good friends. Almond has a thousand stories about Adams. Ott's mother knew that when she died Ott's father would cut him out of his will. When she made her will, therefore, she left her share of the estate to her son. When the will was probated after her death,

2 Denhardt Files, King Ranch Tapes, reel No. 4

Ott's father and brothers were very angry. They did not speak to him for years. Ott had no children. His first wife died, and a second marriage failed. When Ott himself died, he left most of his horses to his hired man, a Mexican-American, and his wife, who had gone to work for him when he grew old. Ott had told them that if they would take care of him until he died he would leave them half of everything he had. The other half he willed to his brothers' grandchildren.

16. The Stallion Without a Name

Ⅰn 1854, soon after Captain King and Legs Lewis started the Santa Gertrudis Ranch, the captain paid $600 for a sorrel stallion named Whirlpool. About two years after Bob Kleberg took over active management of the King Ranch, he paid $125 for a sorrel stallion with no name. The sorrel with a name, Whirlpool, is long forgotten, while the Old Sorrel, who never had a proper name, is famous wherever cowmen gather. In the Old Sorrel, Bob Kleberg had unknowingly acquired the foundation stallion of the King Ranch Quarter Horses. When the sorrel stud colt followed its dam up to the ranch headquarters after a twenty-three-mile walk from Alice, a new era in the King Ranch horse business came with it.

The man who had led the mare and colt to the King Ranch was George Clegg. Clegg had been a premier breeder of Quarter Horses, and the ranch had been watching his progress. Not too long before, Clegg had sent to Illinois for some horse stock, and it was from that blood that the little sorrel colt had come.

George Clegg was interested in horses for two primary purposes: roping and racing. In his younger days, when he ran as many as five thousand head of steers in McMullen, Live Oak, and Duval counties, Clegg went to many ropings near his headquarters in San Diego, Texas. When he became older and the step off the horse seemed farther down, he concentrated more on racing. He had discovered early in life that if you did not have a fast horse you were always going to wind up playing second fiddle, with someone else spending your entry fee or match money. He bought good Quarter Horses and raced good Quarter Horses and rode good Quarter Horses. While racing, he came to know a jockey named Pap Rebo. Rebo had at one time worked for the Little Grove Stock Farm, of Petersburg, Illinois. The owner of the farm was Samuel Watkins, mentioned earlier. Watkins had a reputation throughout the United States as a breeder of fast short-horses.

George Clegg was familiar with the Watkins horses even before he talked to Rebo. He knew about Peter McCue, whom he had seen in San Antonio. He also knew of, and had seen, William Anson's Harmon Baker. When Pap Rebo received a letter from the wife of his former boss, Mrs. Watkins, saying that her husband had died and she was going to sell the horses, Rebo and George put their heads together. George decided that he had better get some of that blood. He wanted a Peter McCue colt like Harmon Baker. Peter McCue's blood was making a name for itself in several sections of Texas, as well as in Oklahoma, Colorado, and New Mexico.

Peter McCue was a half-breed horse. His dam was Nora M. by Voltiguer, a Thoroughbred. His sire was Dan Tucker, whom Tom Trammel had brought to Sweetwater, Texas, from Illinois some years earlier. Dan Tucker was by Barney Owens and out of Butt Cut. Barney was by Cold Deck by Billy Boy by Shiloh and out of a Steel Dust mare. Butt Cut was by Harry Bluff, the sire of Steel Dust, and out of June Bug. Dan Tucker had been foaled on the Little Grove Stock Farm on April 20, 1887. He was a large horse, standing well over fifteen hands and weighing about thirteen hundred pounds.

Peter McCue, Dan Tucker's most famous son, was also a big horse. He stood sixteen hands and weighed over fourteen hundred pounds. Peter was registered as a Thoroughbred under the name Rathnerod, and on his registration papers his sire is listed as the Duke of Highlands. Peter ran most of his races on the smaller tracks in Colorado, Oklahoma, Missouri, and Texas. According to reliable witnesses, at Sportsmen's Park in Chicago he once ran the quarter mile in twenty-one seconds flat. In 1940, when the American Quarter Horse Association was formed, that time appeared a little fantastic, but today it no longer seems impossible.

John Wilkins took Peter McCue to San Antonio, which was his head-quarters from 1907 to 1910. Peter McCue was then sold to Milo Burlington, who stood him at Cheyenne, Oklahoma. In 1915 he was purchased by Si Dawson, who later gave the horse to Coke Roberds, of Hayden, Colorado, where Peter lived out his life, dying in 1923. Peter McCue's sons and daughters are legion and justly celebrated. Some of the better-known offspring are Harmon Baker, John Wilkins, Buck Thomas, Harry D., Duck Hunter, Chief, Jack McCue, Badger, Carrie Nation, and, especially important to this story, Hickory Bill. All of them, except for Hickory Bill, were known to George Clegg and Pap Rebo, and Clegg wrote to Mrs. Watkins telling her what he would like to buy. They finally came to terms on four horses, all purchased to help Clegg's racing and breeding programs. He bought Hickory Bill, Hunter, Lucretia M., and Hattie W.

Hunter was a two-year-old gelding by Hi Henry and out of Hattie W. Hi Henry was out of Butt Cut, the dam of Dan Tucker, and his sire was Peter McCue. Butt Cut was Peter's granddam. Hi Henry had set several track records, running the half mile in 48 seconds, the five-eighths mile in 1 minute, and the three-quarter mile in 1 minute 13¼ seconds. His fastest quarter mile was 22 seconds in a match race when he was carrying 105 pounds. Hunter's dam was Hattie W., whom Clegg also bought. According to the records of the Little Grove Stock Farm, Hattie had a record of 21 seconds, from a running start, for the quarter mile.

Lucretia M. was a bay mare registered by the Jockey Club for racing purposes only, as were many other Watkins horses. The registration certificate shows her to be by The Hero and out of Bird. She was foaled on March 17, 1901. Her greatest claim to fame is that she was the dam of Hickory Bill. On May 10, 1911, when Mrs. Watkins wrote to George Clegg about Hickory Bill, she claimed that the horse had run a quarter mile in 21 seconds, the half mile in 47 seconds, and the five-eighths mile in 1 minute 2 seconds, all on the Chicago track. As a two-year-old, according to what appears to be authentic time, he ran the eighth mile in 10 seconds flat, beating Neverfret, who at that time held at least the track record (and according to Mrs. Watkins the world's record) for the half mile at 46 seconds.

When the time came to collect his new horses, George sent a man to Illinois to ride back with them in the boxcar. When they arrived at the station in Alice, Bob Hunter quoted George as saying: "We had to lead them through town, and they sure caused a lot of excitement. Hickory Bill was a four-year-old then and weighed about 1,150 pounds. He was just about the finest horse people in that part of the country had ever seen."[1]

When George Clegg started breeding Hickory Bill to his Quarter mares, he began to acquire his reputation as a top breeder. George raised a number of outstanding stallions and a dozen or so celebrated mares.

Hickory Bill was registered in the Appendix of *The American Stud Book* as a Thoroughbred. He is also listed in *Sires of American Thoroughbreds*.[2] He was an Appendix horse because his dam, Lucretia M., was out of an unregistered mare named Bird. Bird was a half sister of Steel Dust.[3] George eventually sold Hickory Bill to John Kenedy, of Sarita, who later gave Hickory Bill to Richard Kleberg. According to Clegg, Hickory Bill died in 1921. He caught "Texas fever" when Clegg owned him and lost the sight of one eye.[4] He was completely blind by the time the ranch acquired him, and he had to be hand-bred. He was used mainly on the Laureles Division of the ranch. Nine of his fillies were put into the Quarter Horse broodmare band.

The horse Hunter was the reason George sold Little Joe. George trained Hunter and began racing him. In his fourth race he beat Little Joe. George had had a very good offer for Little Joe from his friend Ott Adams. Another friend, Tom East, was also looking for a Traveler colt. George sold El Rey, Ott's stallion, to East for five hundred dollars and sold Little Joe to Adams for one thousand dollars. Hunter later became stifled but until then ran very well for George.

George bred his Little Joe mares to Hickory Bill and bred the two Watkins mares, Lucretia M. and Hattie W., to Little Joe (he had an agreement with Ott Adams that he could breed a certain number of mares to Little Joe).

1 Bob Hunter, "George Clegg," *Western Livestock Journal,* May, 1941, 17.
2 *Sires of American Thoroughbreds,* 73.
3 Denhardt Files, Michaelis Binders, "Studs E–K."
4 Denhardt Files, Clegg Folder, notes of interview with Helen Michaelis, 1943.

The first colt out of Lucretia was called Joe D (sometimes spelled Jodie and occasionally raced as Jodie Click). Clegg's Joe D turned out to be quite a race horse. He ran some of his most famous races while he was owned by Ernest Lumpkin. Joe D ran against Della Moore three times and beat her twice. He also beat the well-known Little Willie and Alice Blue Gown (Gray Alice). Joe D finally ended up in the hands of Ed Fields, of Richmond, Texas. To his dying day George regretted allowing his trainer to talk him into gelding Joe D.

Hickory Bill started siring top horses right away, and the cross on the Little Joe mares seemed ideal. Some of his better-known sons were Sam Watkins, Little Hickory Bill, O'Conner's Little Hickory, and, of course, the Old Sorrel. The Old Sorrel's dam was not a Little Joe mare.

During the days when Clegg and J. C. McGill were partners in the steer business, Clegg acquired some mares from McGill. McGill had bought a carload of horses from a Dr. Rose, who lived in Del Rio but had ranches in Mexico. When George saw the horses, he was taken with the looks of four of the older mares. He told his partner that he wanted them and said he would replace them with younger mares in better shape. That was fine with McGill, and the trade was made.[5] Clegg then bred Hickory Bill to the mares from Dr. Rose's ranch. One of the mares was the dam of the Old Sorrel, the one George Clegg led to the King Ranch. No other facts are known about the mare, although some assumptions about her can be made.

Dr. Northway, in a speech before the Horse Association of America in December, 1948, had this to say about the dam of the Old Sorrel:

> His mother was supposed to have been a Thoroughbred mare that was bred and raised in Kentucky. Some of you older breeders remember when horses were cheap. A friend of mine in Mexico, a dentist, a Dr. Rose, owned and operated some ranches in Mexico, and as a sideline practiced dentistry in Del Rio, Texas. He was interested in improving his horse stock, so he went to Lexington and bought a carload of mares. I think he got them for $125 each. He took them to Mexico, and they

5 Garford Wilkinson, "George Clegg," *Quarter Horse Journal*, January, 1959, 24.

lost their identity. He turned them out on his ranch. He later became horse-poor and sold a carload to a rancher in Alice, Texas.[6]

From that carload of Kentucky mares came the one that foaled the sorrel stud colt George Clegg led from Alice, the colt that was to start a dynasty in his new home, the Old Sorrel.

[6] "Horse Breeding Operations on the King Ranch" (speech by J. K. Northway, D.V.M., to Horse Association of America, December, 1948), Denhardt Files, Northway Folder, photostat, 8.

17. Foundation Mares—I

WHEN Bob Kleberg decided to breed a better strain of cow horses, he first acquired a stallion, the Old Sorrel. Then he began to collect mares. He began by selecting the best individuals he could find on the ranch. At the same time he began to buy superior Quarter mares to add to his own stock. A carefully selected group provided the base on which the strain was built.

The first crop of colts could trace only to the Old Sorrel on the top line of their pedigree. The second generation, however, traced to the Old Sorrel on their bottom line also. No stallion has been used in the basic program except the Old Sorrel, his sons, and their sons, in direct-line descent. Some outside female blood has been used. Fillies foaled by these outcross horses, when sired by a program stallion, can and do enter the core program. The outcross horses, especially in the early formation years, were an important factor in the success of the King Ranch Quarter Horses.

Certain individuals deserve individual attention. They are the Lazarus mares, Brisa, Water Lilly, Ada Jones, Johnny's Bay, Lady of the Lake, Plain Jane, the Dock Lawrence Mare, the Roan Hickory Bill Mare, Pal, Big Liz, Bill's Liz, Little Liz, High Gear, Verna Grace, Chicara, and Canales Bell. Each is more or less representative of a group of mares with similar ancestors.

LAZARUS MARES

The largest group of mares with common ancestry used in the program in the first few years were ranch mares, all descendants of the Lazarus Thoroughbreds. How the ranch got this excellent group of mares and stallions is an interesting story in itself.

Sam Lazarus lived in Fort Worth before World War I. He started the Acme Cement Company and was successful in other business interests. He became interested in horse racing and then in horse breeding. He was very successful in both pursuits. He stumbled upon some excellent bloodlines that crossed well and produced successful race horses. When racing was outlawed in Texas, however, he had difficulty making his stable pay because of the costs of shipping the horses to and maintaining them at eastern and southern tracks. Then something happened that made him decide to give up racing entirely. A string of his horses who were racing in St. Louis always seemed to break last and maintain their positions. There were unsavory explanations for the poor showing of horses that should have placed in some of the races. He did not like to lose money, and to have it lifted from his pocket was more than he could stand. The situation was especially galling to him because there seemed to be nothing he could do about it. He decided to sell out, race horses, brood mares, stallions, and all.

Lazarus had accumulated one of the better bands of Thoroughbreds outside Kentucky. He knew that some of his erstwhile friends in the racing fraternity would dearly love to get their hands on some of his horses. Most of his mares had a little age on them, and they had produced enough winners that he didn't feel they owed him anything. He decided to see that his horses got good homes in which their excellence would not be wasted—and also to make sure that they and their offspring would not fall into the hands of his former "friends."

Lazarus began to make discreet inquiries about buyers who might be interested in such terms. Someone suggested that the King Ranch was the answer to his requirements. Lazarus called Robert J. Kleberg, Sr., in Corpus Christi and told him that he had some superior horses, thirty mares and two stallions, for sale. Kleberg replied that the ranch was not in the race-horse

94

business and that mares of the quality Lazarus owned were not normally used in cattle operations such as the ranch was pursuing. In short, the ranch was not interested. Lazarus was persistent, however, and finally Kleberg agreed to send someone to Fort Worth to look at the horses. By that time Caesar Kleberg had been working on the ranch for almost ten years, and his knowledge of horses was greatly respected by Kleberg. Caesar was delegated to go to Fort Worth and take a look at Lazarus's Thoroughbreds.

Caesar went to Fort Worth by train, hired a hack near the station, and rode out to the stockyards where the horses were kept. There he met Lazarus, and the two men looked over the horses. Caesar saw that they were of superb quality, worth much more than the ranch would pay for unnecessary horses. After the inspection Lazarus rode back to town with Caesar. Caesar explained that the ranch had several thousand cow horses, as well as top-quality trotting horses for the ranch buggies and carriages, and that the owners were not in the market for more horses. He went on to explain that the ranch had little use for expensive race horses, no matter how good they were. Lazarus said, "I think you will be interested when you hear what I want for them." He had been sizing up Kleberg and had decided that he wanted his horses to go to the King Ranch.

Caesar was astounded when Lazarus offered him kit and caboodle at one hundred dollars a head. Lazarus made only one condition: he did not want the horses registered or raced. Caesar knew good horseflesh when he saw it, and these quality animals were obviously worth ten times the price Lazarus was asking (an ordinary horse was worth almost one hundred dollars at the time). Caesar swung the team around and drove back to the stockyards. He looked over the horses once more and then made arrangements to have them shipped to the ranch.

When Dr. Northway went to the ranch five years later, the two Lazarus stallions had been in the barn for some time and had developed "moon blindness" (periodic ophthalmia). At length it was decided to destroy them. The Lazarus mares, however, provided an invaluable base on which to found a cow-horse program. It should be remembered that when Bob Kleberg started the cow-horse program the aim was not the production of a superior family of Quarter Horses. His main objective was to develop a better cow

95

horse for use on the ranch. It happened that the individual having the characteristics he wanted was a Quarter Horse, the Old Sorrel. The importance Bob Kleberg assigned to the Lazarus blood in his cow-horse program is well illustrated in a ranch memo dated June 24, 1960, from Bob Kleberg to Dick Kleberg:

> In going through some of my old papers I found some pedigrees that were important in our present breed of Quarter Horses.
> MARTINS BEST was a very, very high class Thoroughbred horse that we raised from some of the Sam Lazarus mares. The daughters of this horse, and some of his inbred daughters, were the best mares that were bred to Old Sorrel. His [Martins Best's] whole pedigree is filled with some of the best blood in the world and I thought it would be well to have this preserved with our permanent Quarter Horse records, as the blood of this horse was very important to the foundation of our stud. For instance, the mare Charrita that Lauro [Lauro Cavazos, the ranch foreman] rode and Solis were out of inbred daughters of this horse.[1]

Solis and Little Richard, two of the best King Ranch Quarter Horse stallions, were out of Thoroughbred mares. Solis was out of a Lazarus mare, and Little Richard was out of a Lucky Mose mare.[2]

---

[1] Photostat in Denhardt Files, King Ranch Folder, No. 4. For more about Martins Best, see Chapter 21.

[2] In a letter from Dr. Northway to the author, dated March 22, 1968, the doctor wrote as follows about the Lazarus horses:

"...you asked for more details on the Lazarus and Lucky Mose horses. Bob Kleberg recently told me that the Lucky Mose Thoroughbred Family traced back to Broomstick (TB) and were of the Broomstick Family. Certainly these Lucky Mose horses were top individuals and had wonderful conformation. You will note several of our foundation Quarter Horse sires were out of Lucky Mose mares.

"Bob says that the Lucky Mose blood was crossed on the then existing King Ranch Thoroughbred (not registered) mares.

"The Lazarus mares were consistently bred to Martins Best (TB) by Right Royal (TB). A pedigree of Martins Best was enclosed in our letter of January 29th. You will recall that several of our foundation sires of the Old Sorrel Family were out of Lazarus mares. Bob thinks that Martins Best definitely was probably the best in conformation and type of the early foundation Thoroughbreds that went into this great Family of the Old Sorrel Horse (P-209). That is why I have referred so much to Martins Best in my letters. Bob told me recently that he thought he could locate the original pedigrees of the mares bought from Lazarus. I certainly hope so as this would clear up a lot of conflict.

"It is, of course, true that through time and the passing of years there is some conflict in the

BRISA

Brisa was selected as the first individual mare to be discussed in this chapter for several reasons, not the least being that she was at one time Bob Kleberg's favorite mount. Brisa was not a registered Thoroughbred, but she was clean-bred. Her sire was San Vicente, and her dam was one of the Tod mares.

Brisa was foaled in 1922 and was of an ideal cow-horse conformation, in spite of her Thoroughbred blood. She was of medium stature, with a very muscular though feminine body. She had something else that most Thoroughbreds lack, and that was the ability to work with cattle. She also had an excellent mouth. She made up for any lack of size with her big heart. She didn't know what it meant to give up. If she had been asked, she would have gone until she fell of exhaustion.

With Brisa, Bob Kleberg did all those things a cowman does on horseback. On holidays he took her to rodeos in the region, for she was a top roping and cutting horse. A lot of money was won on her back. She would sometimes carry several different riders in the same show, when Kleberg loaned her to his friends.

Bob Kleberg kept on riding her much longer than he needed to in order to determine that she was good enough to join the Old Sorrel in the breeding program. He simply hated to give her up. Finally she was put in the manada of the Old Sorrel. The next year there were two outstanding stud colts in the pasture, both sired by the Old Sorrel. The foreman, Lauro Cavazos, took a particular liking to one of the colts, a little sorrel he called Melon. Kleberg was attracted to Brisa's colt, which they named Celestino, a name soon shortened to Tino. Bob Kleberg instructed Dr. Northway to watch them carefully until it was time to castrate them. Afterward, Melon was to be

stories, but Mr. Caesar was very definite in his version of what he had bought when he made the trip to Ft. Worth to look at the Lazarus horses and mares. We often referred to the two stallions and 30 mares but never definitely gave their names. This purchase occurred in about 1911 or 1912 following the barring of racing in Texas. You recall that Lazarus requested that the King Ranch not register or race any of the Thoroughbred stock purchased from him. There was no specific horse named Lucky Mose. We referred to them as a group of the Lucky Mose breeding. I do hope that Bob's statement above will help clarify the situation. In other words we had a group we referred to as the Lazarus Mares and a group we referred to as the Lucky Mose Mares." Denhardt Files, Northway Folder.

sent to Lauro, and Tino was to be delivered to Kleberg. Each man would develop his own colt, and they would see which proved the better horse. The colts were to be put through their paces. Dr. Northway said when telling this story, "It was common knowledge that these men were two of the best horsemen in Texas, and both all-around cowboys."[3]

Lauro's colt was by the Old Sorrel and out of a mare recorded as Chicasha Johnson's Chestnut Mare. Both colts broke out well, and both were outstanding in conformation and performance. They took to cattle work, roping and cutting as though they had been doing it always. They could do anything required of a cow horse. It became a contest each time the men rode them into a herd or charged after a calf. It was the very highest type of friendly rivalry, with no quarter asked or given. While the reason for the rivalry was to test the horses and the prepotency of the sire, it was also a contest between owner and top hand. Everyone enjoyed the contest, especially the principals.

Dr. Northway was one of those who watched the rivalry with great interest. He delights in telling stories about the two and about humorous incidents that occurred while they were working with the two horses. One day on a hunting trip Bob Kleberg shot a duck that fell into the middle of a shallow reservoir. He asked his chauffeur, a boy named José Gonzáles, to fetch the duck. José rode Tino into the water to retrieve the bird. When he leaned over to pick it up, the duck, which was still alive, flapped its wings, startling Tino, who threw the boy into the water and trotted back to Kleberg. Tino was not fond of half-dead ducks.

The conformation and ability that Melon and Tino displayed were good indications of the potency of the Old Sorrel. Their high quality went a long way toward convincing Kleberg that the old horse could establish a line of cow horses that would satisfy the high standards he was setting.

Brisa was bred to the Old Sorrel throughout her life. For years she was the bell mare of the Old Sorrel's manada. All told, she produced five bay sons by the Old Sorrel, the first being Tino of the story above. For some reason all of Brisa's colts were called Tino. The next three Tinos were lost by accidents. When she was safely in foal for the fifth time, Bob Kleberg told

[3] Denhardt Files, King Ranch Tapes, reel No. 2.

98

Dr. Northway to bring her in and to see that she safely gave birth. If it was another son, Bob Kleberg was determined to keep him as a stallion.

Brisa was one of the few mares bred to the Old Sorrel that did not produce sorrels. In fact, it was when Bob Kleberg saw how many sorrels the Old Sorrel was producing that he decided to try to set that color along with the other characteristics. He felt that it would be fitting to work the red Santa Gertrudis cattle with red horses. But the second surviving Tino was so exceptional that Kleberg ignored the rule in his case, and he was one of the few sons of the Old Sorrel that was kept and bred despite his bay color. Other nonsorrels showed up occasionally, such as Comanche and Smoky, but they were seldom used as stallions. The same is true of the second- and third-generation horses. With a very few exceptions,[4] all stallions used were sorrel.

WATER LILLY

Water Lilly, registered number 168 by the American Quarter Horse Association, was as good a Quarter mare as the King Ranch ever owned, especially when it came to producing. She would have been notable if she had produced only Hired Hand. However, she foaled other great stallions, such as Little Man, and such mares as Little Water Lily and Lady Speck. Lady Speck was one of the fastest mares that ever ran on the short tracks of South Texas. The only mare that may have been faster was Miss Princess. Lady Speck and Miss Princess lived a generation apart, however, and they were never matched. Miss Princess always ran honest, doing her best each time. Her best was the best, and she was the World Champion Quarter Horse. Lady Speck, on the other hand, ran only fast enough to win. She was satisfied simply to beat her opponents. That is why a comparison of their times does not tell too much.

In 1939, Bob Kleberg agreed to run Don Manners, a ranch-bred Thoroughbred, against Lady Speck for a quarter mile. Kleberg did not know too much about Lady Speck, but he did know that Don Manners could run. He had heard that Lady Speck had beaten Cyclone in three straight races.

[4] The exceptions are Señor Dulce, dun; Wimpy's Greylake, gray; Candy K, bay; Leacho, bay; Reganio, bay; and Tipo de Norias, bay.

After the third win Cyclone's backers finally saw the light, even though Lady Speck had just nudged him out. Cyclone was no pushover. He was a bay gelding who had been sired by Alamo by Uncle Jimmy Gray. His dam was reported to have been a daughter of Alamo. On several occasions Cyclone ran in creditable times on tracks recognized by Melville Haskill's American Quarter Racing Association. He beat 23 seconds in the quarter and had an official 350 yards in 18½ seconds. Perhaps these are not world's-record times, but it certainly would take a race horse to better them.

Lady Speck was sired by Major Speck when he was standing at John Kenedy's ranch at Sarita. Kenedy later sold her to Esteban García, of McAllen. She was a sorrel mare, standing on some little leg, and weighed in training about one thousand pounds. Will Hysaw, known wherever race men gathered, said that she was out of a Yellow Jacket mare, Water Lilly. At the time Lady Speck was matched against Don Manners she was being raced by Sheriff Cardway, of Kenedy County.

Don Manners was a Thoroughbred stallion sired by Lovely Manners, an Army Remount Service stallion kept by Richard Kleberg for a time. Lovely Manners was by Sweep. Don Manners was out of Chicaro Jane, a daughter of Chicaro and Katie Dale. He was a medium-sized Thoroughbred, but very smooth, with good bone and deep through the heart. He was a bay, with a small star and three white feet. He was foaled in 1936 and showed great promise from the start.

The person who had had the race matched was John Kenedy, Bob Kleberg's neighbor and friendly rival. John asked Bob to judge the race, and Bob had to decide the race against his own horse. It was won by the shortest of noses, which added greatly to John's pleasure. Lady Speck ran her usual race and barely beat Don Manners at the finish. Actually, if there had been a photo finish, it might have been a tie—it was that close. A picture of the race tells the story. A man is shown standing on the fence with his arms spread out and his shoulders hunched up, expressing as clearly as words, "Now who can tell how that race went?" The horses ran the quarter in 22¾ seconds.

Water Lilly was Lady Speck's dam. Dr. Northway had purchased Water Lilly in 1934, about four years before the race described above, for two

100

hundred dollars. Henry Seiler, who owned her at the time, was in a jackpot. A so-called friend had left one hundred gallons of bootleg whisky in his barn, and Henry had been caught with it. Henry, needing money to get out of the predicament, called Bob Kleberg to see whether he could sell him a horse. Kleberg asked Dr. Northway to look at the horses.

The doctor did not like the looks of the filly that Seiler wanted to sell him and said so. He did like the look of an old sorrel mare in the same pen, however, and offered to buy her. At first Henry said no; then, remembering his need for cash, he agreed to sell her but asked for her unborn foal. Northway bought the mare and took her to the ranch. The next day he thought it over and decided that Bob Kleberg would not approve of the arrangement and that he had better buy the foal too. Seiler wanted one hundred dollars for the foal, but Northway felt that was too much; one could buy a well-broken horse for that amount in the 1930's. He mailed Seiler a check for sixty-five dollars, figuring that Seiler would accept it. He did so, and the ranch had Water Lilly and her foal.

Later that spring the foal, a filly, was dropped and was named Little Water Lily.[5] Little Water Lily had been sired by a Remount stallion by the name of Lion D'Or. Lion D'Or had been standing in San Antonio at Ed Pfefferling's Horse and Mule Barn (where Uncle Jimmy Gray also stood). Lion D'Or was by Heno by Henry Young and out of Aile D'Or by Captain Hancock. Both Henry Young and Captain Hancock were grandsons of *Leamington.[6] The King Ranch had three mares by Lion D'Or: Little Liz, Roan Liz, and Little Water Lily.

Water Lilly was foaled in 1920, and various accounts of her breeding have been given. When she was growing up, Quarter mares were not considered very valuable unless they could run fast, and even then they were worth only a few hundred dollars. When they could not race any more, they were of little value, and no one paid much attention to their breeding. Moreover, many race-horse men found it more convenient not to have a pedigree

[5] Little Water Lily is carried in the *AQHA Stud Book* as having being foaled in 1940. It would seem that if she was by Lion D'Or, Little Water Lily was the first of Water Lilly's foals born on the ranch, and so was actually born in 1934.

[6] An asterisk preceding the name of a Thoroughbred indicates that the horse has been imported.

101

for their short-horses. A horse of unknown parentage was easier to match, especially if the sire happened to be a well-known producer of speed. By the time Water Lilly was purchased by Dr. Northway, she had been through several hands, and the later owners had bought her for her looks and not for her pedigree. Consequently, Henry Seiler was unable to give the doctor much information about her background.

When Jim Minnick, Lee Underwood, and I arrived at the King Ranch in 1940 to inspect and register the first group of ranch horses for the American Quarter Horse Association, we accepted Water Lilly. She was by that time twenty years old but looked half that age. She was a dark sorrel, with the exception of a white saddle mark on the left side of her withers. She had everything a Quarter mare needed: good bone, straight legs, a deep sloping hip, a short back, good withers, a feminine neck, and a good head. The way she worked her little fox ears all the time would make one think she could hear a cloud passing overhead.

Since nothing was known for certain of her ancestry, she was registered as having an unknown sire and dam. Her conformation and the conformation of her offspring left no doubts in our minds that she deserved registration. Some years later, after Helen Michaelis had replaced me as secretary of the AQHA, Bob Kleberg found out how she was probably bred. Will ("Red") Hysaw, a race-horse man with a knife-sharp memory, said that Water Lilly had been sired by Waggoner's Yellow Jacket. Hysaw had known Water Lilly when she was racing. Other indications also pointed to that breeding. The information was forwarded to the association, and her registry was amended to show that she was by Yellow Jacket.

Yellow Jacket was a dun horse with a light-red mane and tail. He was a little over fourteen–three hands high and a typical hard-twisted Quarter Horse stallion. If Water Lilly was indeed by Yellow Jacket, she was well bred and was a half sister to Cowboy, who sired Shue Fly and Hard Twist. Yellow Jacket was by Rondo.

On that first AQHA inspection trip, Lee Underwood recognized Water Lilly's brand as one belonging to the Waggoners. He later talked to Lige Reed about the mare. Lige had been connected with the Waggoners' Quarter Horse program in the 1920's, and if anyone knew the answer he did. After talking with other old Three D hands, Reed finally said that most likely a mare so branded would have been sired by Buck Thomas and not by Yellow Jacket. Water Lilly may therefore have been by Buck Thomas. Like Yellow Jacket, Buck Thomas was well bred. The Waggoners did not keep any stallions that were not.

Buck Thomas was sired by the famous Peter McCue and was a half brother of Hickory Bill, the sire of the King Ranch's Old Sorrel. Buck Thomas also sired Bill Thomas, who was owned by Jack Hutchins of the Shanghai Pierce Estate, at Wharton, Texas. Buck Thomas was bred by Coke Roberds, of Hayden, Colorado, who sold him to the Waggoners.

Regardless of the exact breeding of Water Lilly, the King Ranch never had reason to regret buying her. Before the American Quarter Horse Association was organized, her bloodlines were not important. Water Lilly had the conformation they were looking for, and she produced the kind of colts they wanted, with speed and cow sense.

Water Lilly's first foal born on the ranch, Little Water Lily, was ridden until she proved her ability and was then returned to the breeding program. She produced some outstanding daughters, including Sandia de Chale, Larguita, Sandia Lily, Pascuas Lirio, and Acuarela. Her stud colts were, with one exception, gelded and ridden by the Kineños.

After Little Water Lily was foaled, Water Lilly was bred to Chicaro. The result of that union was a bay filly foaled in the spring of 1935, which was named Delicatesa de Texas. In 1939, bred to Chicaro, Delicatesa foaled Chic Tex Pride. Water Lilly did not have a stud colt until 1941, when she foaled Little Man. Little Man, by the Old Sorrel, received his name because, although he was small, he looked like bees had stung him all over—he was all man. He performed beautifully when broken and ridden, and Bob Kleberg put him back into the breeding program as a stallion. He was used by the ranch from 1944 until 1955 and sired some of the very best mares now in use.

Water Lilly failed to foal in 1942. She had once more been bred to Chicaro in hopes that she would produce a race horse, but she didn't catch and was barren that year. Had she produced a foal, it might have been something.

When Water Lilly again failed to conceive in 1942, it was decided to return her to the Old Sorrel and try for another stud colt. Water Lilly was getting old, as was the Old Sorrel. The next year, in 1943, she foaled Hired Hand, one of the last stallions sired by the Old Sorrel, and his greatest.

18. Foundation Mares—II

T<small>HERE</small> are many interesting stories about other foundation mares —too many to tell them all. Some, however, deserve a paragraph or two, even though they are not individually as important as Water Lilly or Brisa or collectively as influential as the Lazarus mares. Three of this group were by Little Joe, premier sire of South Texas Quarter Horses. They were Ada Jones, Lady of the Lake, and Plain Jane.

A<small>DA</small> J<small>ONES</small>

Ada Jones was a roan sorrel with a bald face and a white hind leg. In fact, she had so much white on her that it would probably be difficult to register her today. If one ignored her coloration, however, she had everything. There is an old snapshot of Ada taken back in the early 1920's. She is being held by Ott Adams, her breeder. On the back of the snapshot is the following, signed O. S. Adams (but written by his first wife):

> Ada Jones was sired by Little Joe her dam was Mamie Crowder of racing fame. Mamie was sired by Old Jno. Crowder, her mother was a Blue Eye mare owned by Will Shely. Ada made good in Kenedy Fair meet defeating a fast bunch of horses going ⅜ mile on a heavy track time 39 sec. Her first race 30 days from the time she was broken to ride. Mighty good her first race.[1]

1 Denhardt Files, Ada Jones Folder.

Ada was foaled in 1918 and was raised by Adams. She was sold to the King Ranch in 1934 by John Dial. Her first foal on the ranch was Cambiada, who was sired by Chicaro. In 1938 she foaled John Dial, also by Chicaro. She produced only fillies when bred to the Old Sorrel. Ada Jones was also the dam of Chicaro's Hallie, who was foaled while Ada was owned by John Dial. Ada died April 30, 1941. One could write a book about Chicaro Hallie's Thoroughbred produce.[2] Ada's blood was truly prepotent.

LADY OF THE LAKE

Lady of the Lake and Johnny's Bay came to the King Ranch with John Armstrong when he was hired by Bob Kleberg to help with the short-horses. Johnny's Bay was a beautiful dark bay. She had a star, and both feet on the left side had white, and she sported a few roan hairs on her hips. She was sired by Paul El and was out of a Little Joe mare. She went to the ranch in 1935 but was not bred until 1944, when she foaled a filly sired by Wimpy.

Lady of the Lake was by Little Joe, one of the very few gray horses he is known to have sired. Of the 114 colts recorded as sired by Little Joe, bays and sorrels predominated, followed by browns, blacks, and roans. Only two are listed as gray, and only one as a paint.[3]

As mentioned earlier, John Armstrong raced Lady of the Lake for a number of years.[4] Her first foal arrived in 1936, when she produced Black Lake after being bred to the Old Sorrel. After Black Lake she produced a string of fillies until 1945, when she foaled Wimpy's Greylake. Lady of the Lake was as good a Quarter mare as I have ever seen. She had a beautiful head and a feminine neck and was deep through the heart. She had a straight leg under every corner, and her knees were close to the ground. She had a

[2] Chicaro's Hallie's daughters founded a dynasty of sprinters. Chicaro's Hallie was a winner at two years, winning her first race, as did Bruja, her daughter, and Woven Web (Miss Princess), her granddaughter. Bruja had four fabulous daughters: Encantadora, a winner at 2, setting a world's record for 5 furlongs of .57 flat; Haunted, a stakes winner, who set a new world's record at Golden Gate Fields, 4½ furlongs in .52 flat; Witchbrew (better known as Mickie on the short tracks), who ran an official 350 yards in .18 flat and was the dam of winners; and Woven Web (also known as Miss Princess), who equaled the world's record for 2½ furlongs in .27 1/5 and set the world's record quarter mile standing start at .22 flat. Baloma, daughter of Woven Web, also held track records. That was a real sprinting family.

[3] Denhardt Files, Michaelis Binders, "Unregistered Get," 1844–1945.

[4] See page 77.

colt almost every year until she became arthritic at twenty-four and Dr. Northway had to destroy her.

PLAIN JANE

Plain Jane was a bay mare, foaled in 1927. She too was bred by Ott Adams and was by Little Joe and out of Mamie Roberts by Ace of Hearts. She was owned by Ed Rachel, of Falfurrias, Texas, when the ranch acquired her.[5] Ed owned a lot of good mares and never seemed to have enough grass. He was good-hearted and loaned many mares to his friends to keep and breed. That is how John Dial got several of his Little Joe mares, including Plain Jane. When Bob Kleberg found out how well the blood of Little Joe was crossing with the Old Sorrel, he was eager to obtain as many Little Joe mares as he could. He asked Dr. Northway to talk to Ed Rachel. Ed said that he would not sell Plain Jane but told the doctor to go to John Dial's, take her, and use her.

Plain Jane's daughter, Alazana de Adan, sired by Babe Grande, also left some good progeny. She was born in 1943 and was first bred to Wimpy's Greylake and then to several other stallions. In all she produced five fillies and four colts. Her last filly, Adana de Texas, was sent to the King Ranch Australian division. Her last colt was foaled in 1962.

THE DOCK LAWRENCE MARE

The mare that the ranch always referred to as the Dock Lawrence Mare

[5] In a letter to the author, dated March 15, 1968, Doc Northway wrote as follows: "Ed Rachel was one of the best fellows in the world, but he was usually overstocked with horses and cattle. Being big hearted he would lend his livestock to friends gratuitously, and many of them did borrow stallions or mares from Ed. At one time Plain Jane (1229) was in the hands of John Dial, who bred her to some of his own stallions. You will recall that later two of her descendants were given to the Ranch by John Dial. I think the ownership was always a little doubtful between Ed Rachel and John Dial because they were good friends and handled their business deals rather loosely, but the two mares did come to the Ranch as a gift to Bob Kleberg from John Dial. One was named Silva's Brown Mare and the other went to Norias and was never registered as a Quarter mare.

"Anyway Ed Rachel did not want to sell Plain Jane (1229), but told Bob he would lend her to him. We brought her here in 1943 and bred her to the Old Sorrel Horse in May of 1943. She was not in too good physical shape, and we tried to build her up. In 1944 she was bred to Babe Grande (P-205) and foaled a chestnut filly Alazana de Adan (App.) on May 18, 1945. Unfortunately Plain Jane (1229) got down. I kept her supported in an equine swing for some time but eventually lost her 8/13/45." Denhardt Files, Northway Folder. Ranch records show that Alanza de Adan was born not in 1945 but in 1943.

was one of its very top mares. She was also the dam of two of the outstanding stallions used in the Quarter Horse breeding program, Tomate Laureles and Baby Chiquito. This mare was purchased in 1926 at the suggestion of Bob Kleberg's sister Sarah. She and a few friends, including Dr. Northway, had gone to Alice for a little race meet to be held in George Clegg's cotton field. It was just a neighborhood get-together, and the races were run down the old cotton rows. Those who matched the race would tell the finish judge how far to go down the row to end the race. The horses were started by the lap-and-tap system, with the starter tapping them off if they were closely lapped when they passed him.

One man was racing an extremely good-looking mare. He was a self-trained veterinarian by the name of Lawrence, a well-known and colorful figure. He had lost a leg and had a crutch strapped around the stump and anchored to a belt around his waist. If his artificial leg slowed him down any, it wasn't noticeable. Since before World War I, Lawrence had had a good practice in Jim Wells County. Dr. Northway aptly described his colleague when he said, "With all due respect to the dead, he was quite a wind-jammer."

Sarah Kleberg liked Lawrence's mare so well that she asked Dr. Northway to try to buy her for the ranch. He did so, at a price of $160, and from that day on she was always referred to as the Dock Lawrence Mare. She was by Little Joe and out of a Hickory Bill mare. In 1927 the ranch bred her to the Old Sorrel, and she produced Tomate Laureles. Tomate was used in the Quarter Horse program for many years, as was one of her later colts, Baby Chiquito, and her fillies.

Babe Grande is listed in the *AQHA Stud Book* as being out of the Dock Lawrence Mare.[6] That is a mistake. Babe Grande's dam was bred somewhat similarly, but they were not the same. Babe Grande's dam was a Hickory Bill mare, and, because she was never named and was a roan, she was carried in the books of the ranch and referred to as the Roan Hickory Bill Mare. Her dam was Mamie J, a daughter of Mamie Crowder.

6 "Babe Grande No. 113—Ch. S. 1928; King Ranch, Kingsville, Texas; Sarah Kleberg, Kingsville, Texas; sire, Old Sorrel by Hickory Bill by Peter McCue; dam, Dr. Lawrence mare by Strickland Horse by Hickory Bill." *Official Stud Book and Registry of the American Quarter Horse Association* (Fort Worth, 1941), I, 62.

Bob Kleberg and George Clegg were driving around one Sunday after-noon when they bought a roan Quarter mare. George told Kleberg that he knew where a good mare could be found. Kleberg, always interested in good mares, suggested that they drive by to see her. George Clegg always had a few mares "farmed out" to other breeders or ranchers. He raised more than he could feed, and the deal was that the horse belonged to the man who was keeping her but that if Clegg could sell her they would split the profit. The roan Quarter mare had been farmed out at Agua Dulce under such terms. Kleberg and Clegg drove down to Agua Dulce, and Kleberg bought the mare. In 1923 she foaled Babe Grande after being bred to the Old Sorrel.[7]

PAL

Uncle Jimmy Gray had a profound influence on the short-running horses all over the Southwest, and it is not surprising to find some of his blood on the King Ranch. Uncle Jimmy had had an illustrious racing career that took him from Oklahoma to New Orleans and elsewhere, and when his racing days were over, the Army Remount Service acquired him for their program. All his Remount Service years were spent in San Antonio at Ed Pfefferling's stables.

One of the very best King Ranch mares, Pal, was by Alamo, a son of Uncle Jimmy Gray. Not too much else is known of Pal's background. She was a beautiful black mare with a small white star on her forehead. Her only other marks were a little white on the inside of the right rear coronet and a barbed-wire scar on one front leg. Pal was purchased by Bob Kleberg from a short-horse man from San Antonio, who brought her to the Kingsville rodeo and race meet in 1936. Kleberg saw her, liked her looks, and sent one of the boys around to see whether she could be bought. The owner said that she was being entered in a six-hundred-dollar claiming race and that if someone wanted her he could claim her. Kleberg did so.

Pal was bred to the Old Sorrel, and in 1937 she foaled Negra Ingrata. Negra in turned foaled three of the top mares of the day: Papa de Adan,

---

[7] Letter from Dr. Northway to the author, dated February 8, 1968, Denhardt Files, North-way Folder.

Gordonis, and Sin Verguenza. In 1939, Pal foaled the famous and aptly named Nobody's Friend (it seemed that most of the Jimmy Grays were a little hardheaded). Nobody's Friend was a sensation when he raced in Tucson in 1942. Like all of Pal's progeny, he matured into a heavily muscled horse. As mentioned earlier, in the world's championship race in Tucson in 1942 he was edged by a nose in the quarter mile by the great Shue Fly. In 1940, Pal produced Border Patrol; in 1944, Wim Pal; in 1945, Peppy Kleberg; in 1948, La Bruja Negra; and in 1950, Pal Chiquita.

BIG LIZ

Bill's Liz, Roan Liz, and Little Liz were the daughters of Big Liz, all good horses. The ancestry of Big Liz is somewhat clouded, like that of so many of the foundation animals of the Quarter Horse breed, all of whom lived a number of years before the AQHA was organized. Helen Michaelis made a concerted effort to trace Big Liz's ancestry, and the following account is taken from her notes.

In a letter written in 1945, Ott Adams reported that someone in San Antonio who owned Nettie Harrison sent her to Bill Nack to be bred to Paul El. Nettie had her colt, a filly they called Big Liz, and died at Nack's. Bill Nack kept Big Liz and never reported that Nettie had had a filly.

Fourteen miles west of Goliad is the little settlement of Berclair, where George Groll lived and kept horses. According to both Will Hysaw and John Armstrong, Groll acquired Big Liz and raced her for a few years. Then she was bred, and, according to Mamie Benevides, her first filly was also a running horse, named Pitchin Sis. Sometime later Tom Burns, of Yoakum, bought Big Liz and a few years afterward sold her to Bob Kleberg. Two daughters of Big Liz were also purchased by the ranch, Roan Liz and Little Liz.[8] Roan Liz, who was foaled in 1939, was by Lion D'Or. Big Liz was then bred back to Lion D'Or and in 1940 foaled Little Liz. Big Liz was then bred to Chicaro Bill again and foaled Bill's Liz on the ranch in 1941. Big Liz and her daughters were all excellent producers for the ranch.

[8] Denhardt Files, Michaelis Binders, "Mares A–Z."

110

High Gear

High Gear was one of the top King Ranch mares. She was sired by Magician, who was by Rainy Day, and she was out of Mamie Hogett by Captain Joe by Traveler. Captain Joe was bred by Will Shely. High Gear was bred by Will Wingate, of Devine, Texas. Tom Garrett, of Devine, claimed that High Gear was out of the same dam as Clabber, which is interesting if true. At one time Garrett owned High Gear. She was then sold to Jim Crutchfield, of San Antonio, who in turn sold her to Bob Kleberg in 1936. Details of that sale are found elsewhere in the book.

High Gear was a medium-sized mare, a bright sorrel with a small star. She was foaled in 1928 and was eight years old when Kleberg bought her. She had a split right ear, which made her easy to identify. She contributed more than her share to the King Ranch program. She was the dam of Coquena, Panda de High Gear, Overdrive, Tamo, and Kingwood. Overdrive was the dam of Hand Drive, Stick, and Repetidas Veces. Kingwood was sold as a yearling to R. L. Underwood, of Wichita Falls, and his blood was in great demand in North Texas and Oklahoma.

Verna Grace

Another of the King Ranch's good Little Joe mares was Verna Grace. She was a beautiful bay mare, somewhat long in the back and about fourteen–one or fourteen–two hands high. She had a star and a streak, socks on her rear legs, and a white place above her left front heel. She was foaled in 1926 and was by Little Joe, and her dam was Johnny Wilkins. Johnny Wilkins was by Horace H, and Verna Grace's second dam was a Thoroughbred mare owned by John Wilkins, of San Antonio, the same Wilkins who owned Peter McCue for a time. Verna Grace was originally called Fair Chance, but when John Armstrong bought and raced her, he renamed her Verna Grace. Armstrong later sold her to John Dial. Dial bred her to the Thoroughbred Chicaro and got Chicaro Bill (who had quite a history of his own). In 1935, Dial sold Verna Grace to Bob Kleberg. Her first foal on the ranch was a filly named Bernice. In 1940 she foaled Rosa Linda, and in 1941, La Rosita de Verna Grace.

111

CHICARA

The ranch also obtained Chicara from John Dial. She was sired by Chicaro. She was a bay, foaled in 1934. The ranch purchased her in 1938. Her dam was a good Ace of Hearts mare owned by John Dial. She is best remembered for her filly Winny de Beto, who was the dam of King Hand, Toronja Winnie, Chalupa, and Wimpa Cardina.

CANALES BELL

Canales Bell, another top mare, was one of about ten mares that Richard Kleberg and George Clegg bought from the Canales Ranch. On one or two occasions Richard Kleberg and George Clegg owned some horses jointly, and this was one of the occasions. The Canales people ranched just across the west fence line from the King Ranch, branding a 22 on the left shoulder. Like the Klebergs, they were friendly with another neighboring rancher, Anastachio Saenz, who was generally known as Tacho Saenz.

One of the horses Kleberg and Clegg owned together gained some fame in the early 1920's. Fred Post, one of the best polo players of his day, suddenly found that he needed one more horse for the playoff between England and the United States. He called Kleberg and asked him whether he had a likely prospect. Richard Kleberg said that he had one mare that might serve the purpose—one of the Canales mares that was working out well. She performed admirably for Post and became one of his favorite ponies.

Canales Bell, born in 1923, was sired by Roan Clegg, a son of Hickory Bill, and out of Pelicana, who was by Texas Chief and out of a descendant of Mamie Crowder. Like so many of the outcross mares, she was royally bred. She was a light sorrel with a flax mane and tail and roan hairs in her flanks. She was bred to the Old Sorrel, and produced China, Silver Lucy, and Macanudo. Macanudo was one of the first of the ranch Quarter Horse stallions (along with Peppy and Wimpy) to gain nationwide recognition. All of them won performance and conformation shows during the late 1930's and early 1940's.

112

PYLE MARES

The Pyle Dun Mare was another grand brood mare obtained by the ranch. Early in 1921, when the King Ranch initiated the tick-eradication program, Bob Kleberg anticipated the need of additional horses. The men were going to have to gather cattle every fifteen days. Later the period was changed to every eighteen days, which gave the hands a little more time to gather cattle on the different divisions. To supply the extra horses, Kleberg bought approximately forty cow ponies from the Pyle Ranch. The Pyle horses were somewhat different in type from most of the King Ranch horses, which showed considerable Thoroughbred blood. They were good, stocky, well-built horses.[9]

One of the Pyle mares proved to be an exceptional individual. She was always referred to as the Pyle Dun Mare. She was a natural all-around cow horse. Dr. Northway tells an amusing story about this mare:

On this particular day, Bob wanted me to ride this dun P mare.

[9] The stallion Señor Dulce traces back to these horses, and it was from them that he got his dun coat. Some of the dun color found in the King Ranch horses, especially those at the East Ranch at Hebbronville, go back to Grano de Oro, a horse that came from Mexico. Others in this group include Pato and Chivo. The East horses were so colorful that several Wallace Beery pictures with Mexican backgrounds, such as *Pancho Villa*, were filmed on the East Ranch. One of the better-known Hebbronville stallions that were raised on the King Ranch property was Lobo. He was sired by Lovely Manners, but his dam, the Pyle Dun Mare by East's Yellow Jacket, was prepotent enough to give him a dun coat. The Pyle Dun Mare was out of one of the Pyle mares.

Dr. Northway described the Pyle mares as follows: "They were very uniform in conformation, duns, grullos, sorrels—pretty good horses. One of those mares we called the Pyle Dun Mare; Bob took [her] over for his special mount and trained [her] for cutting and roping. She was a pretty darned good mare, but I knew she would break in two, and I was always a little fearful of her. Bob rode her for a number of years, cutting cattle and roping on her. One Fourth of July we all went down to Falfurrias—the American Legion used to have a big rodeo down there. We were all having a good time. Bob was going to rope off the dun mare. She was as quick as a streak of lightning. Well, Mr. Caesar was always liking to play a joke on somebody. So he worked for some time trying to get things just right. He started agitating which horse I was going to ride, and this and that. On this particular day I was to ride a red roan mare that was a mount of Epps Godwin, who was a top cowman and good roper, and this mare would run just as straight and level as an arrow. I'm left-handed, and it didn't make any difference to her if you roped off the right side or the left. She would put you right up there, and if you didn't catch the calf, it was your fault. So I was all lined up to use this mare. The interesting thing about it was that Mr. Caesar was always big-hearted. He said he would pay my entry fee, and then the sly old duck would bet against me. And he would make several bets and come out ahead." Denhardt Files, King Ranch Tapes, reel No. 3.

She had a P for Pyle branded on her thigh. I said, "No, thank you, I don't believe I want to ride her."

Finally he said, "Why don't you want to ride her?"

I didn't want anything to happen before this crowd. I had a lot of friends down there, Fourth of July celebration, and all of the ranch people, Legion boys and everyone.

"What are you going to ride?" he wanted to know.

"I'm going to ride Goodwin's mare."

"Well," he said, "she's no good. Take my P mare."

I said, "Bob, I've seen her break in two, and I don't want her to spill me right in front of this crowd of people."

"Aw—she won't do anything."

"Well, that's my opinion."

"What makes you think so?" he said.

"I've seen her break in two," I said.

Well, sir, the McGill brothers, good friends of the King Ranch, Frank and Claude, came along. They were operating two ranches at the time. One was the Schaffer Ranch north of Alice, and they had the Santa Rosa Ranch. Frank and Claude McGill and Tom East, early in their careers, bought and sold lots of livestock. So they had Jack Terrell on the Santa Rosa Ranch, and he ran it very much like the old-time ranches, and so did Seth Woods down here. They were the *patróns*. The ranch workers would come to them, and they would give their personal checks, and at the end of the month they would come in and settle up. So that continued on for 25 or 30 years before one retired and the other died. Anyway, Jack Terrell was with them. He was heavier than I am and almost as short, pot-gutted, but a good roper and rider.

It seemed that everything was going good and everyone was feeling fine. He said, "Aw—Mr. Bob, Mr. Bob, do me a favor."

Bob said, "Sure."

"Lend me a horse, lend me a horse."

"Sure, sure," said Bob. "Saddle up the dun mare. Do you have a saddle, Jack?"

"Nope, I don't have a saddle or a horse."

"Well," said Bob, "Doc's saddle ought to fit you. Is it all right with you, Doc?"

"Sure," I said.

So the boys put my saddle on the dun P mare, led her around a few minutes. Jack was nervous and thought they were calling him to rope. So we got him mounted, and he backed the little old mare into the chute. The calf broke, and the mare broke, and when Jack leaned over to throw that rope, she broke in two. Man alive, he was out of the saddle, in front of the saddle, behind the saddle, and wound up around her neck holding onto it for dear life. We just stood there watching.

Bob said, "Well, I guess I have just lost a friend."

I said, "Yes, Mr. Kleberg, you have not only just lost a friend, but you are the president and general manager of the King Ranch, and you own that mare. You are going to have to ride that mare."

He says, "Get your saddle off of her and put mine back on. I want to get her back out there and ride her." He got out there, and when they called his name, he came out and won the roping on that little mare. She was the mother of Comanche. Comanche was bred consistently on the Norias Division, and was a dun.[10]

Bob Kleberg is of the opinion that the Pyle horses trace back to Yellow Wolf.[11] No official breeding can be given for the Pyle Dun Mare, but many of the best ranch horses carry her in their pedigree.

[10] Denhardt Files, King Ranch Tapes, reel No. 3. See also letter from Bob Kleberg, dated May 20, 1969, King Ranch Folder No. 3.
[11] Letter from Dr. Northway, dated March 22, 1968, Denhardt Files, Northway folder.

19. The Old Sorrel Fits In

THE last of the Thoroughbreds to come to the ranch from the Remount Service as a prospective sire of cow horses was Lovely Manners, who was by Sweep. Lovely Manners was a good individual, as were some of his sons, such as Don Manners. Earlier there had been hopes for *Naughty Boy II, a Remount Service horse imported from France; but *Naughty Boy II was somewhat on the leggy side, and his colts showed little promise as cow horses.

His son, Naughty Boy III, however, suited Bob's wife, Helen Kleberg, who loved hunters and jumpers. Mrs. Kleberg had supervised the construction of a jumping course on the ranch. When completed, the course was good enough to serve for Olympic equestrian trials. She was sure that Naughty Boy III was going to breed some jumpers worthy of the course.

As the story goes, after the course was completed, Mrs. Kleberg asked her husband to look it over. After looking at it, Bob said to his wife, half teasingly, "I have a plain old cow horse that could jump those things." Mrs. Kleberg looked skeptical, and Kleberg asked a Kineño standing nearby to bring up the Old Sorrel. The Old Sorrel was led from the barn, and someone asked Kleberg which saddle he wanted. He said, "Never mind the saddle," and swung up on the horse bareback, with just the halter rope looped around the stallion's neck. Up and over he went around the course, clearing the

116

highest bar—four feet—with ease. It was the first and last time the Old Sorrel traveled a jumping course.

"How did you know that horse would jump?" asked Mrs. Kleberg, surprised by the horse's ability. "It was easy," said Bob. "The way he can jump prickly pear and mesquite showed he would have no trouble on this easy footing." This story of an incident that happened almost forty years ago gives a good insight into the ability of the Old Sorrel—and also of his master, for that matter.

The story is also reminiscent of something Bob Kleberg's daughter Helenita told me in the summer of 1966, when I was visiting the family on the Norias Division. Speaking of her childhood, she said: "Dad put my Thoroughbred mare in the Quarter Horse mare band. He told me that crossing Thoroughbred to Thoroughbred just came out bad for a good ranch horse. He said to me, 'Isn't it wonderful, when you breed a Thoroughbred to a Quarter Horse, how they come out sound?' "[1]

During World War I the ranch was shorthanded. To further complicate matters, rumors of violence were in the air—threats that boded ill to the Nueces strip. Bandits from south of the border were riding again, just as they had in Captain King's time. That was also the time when Bob Kleberg decided that the ranch should try one of George Clegg's best stud colts. He had seen and had been impressed by one colt in particular, a good-looking sorrel with two small white marks, a star and a snip under the right nostril. Kleberg asked his cousin Caesar, who was assistant general manager of the ranch at the time, to buy the horse at the first opportunity.

Not long afterward Caesar went to Alice with Tom East to buy steers. On the way home they stopped to look at Clegg's horses and mares. Caesar bought the sorrel colt Kleberg wanted, and George delivered it.[2]

Up to that point the sorrel colt simply represented another hope. Like so many other horses bought by the ranch, only time would tell his worth. As the colt matured, however, respect for his beautiful conformation grew. When they first began to ride him, he was given the same training and treatment that all King Ranch cow horses receive. It was a rough, tough training,

[1] Notes made July 11, 1966, Denhardt Files, King Ranch Folder No. 3.
[2] Letter from Bob Kleberg, dated May 20, 1969, Denhardt Files, Kleberg Folder No. 3.

117

hard work and hard play. He learned the feel of a *vaquero's* quirt, the spur, and the rude shock of a steer flipping at the end of the rope he was holding. He grew accustomed to cactus, sand, and thorny brush, to dust, heat, and sweat. He was like any cow horse—only better. Dr. Northway said:

> I saw Richard Kleberg and George Clegg rope off him and ride him all morning and then race him in the afternoon. Although a stallion and treated as such, his daily work consisted of regular ranch routine with the remuda. Bob had made him into a superior cow horse in every respect. You could rope, cut, or do any other ranch work on him, and he was not just adequate—he was superior in all his actions.[3]

All the key ranch hands liked to ride the sorrel stallion because he could do everything—and do it better than the other horses. Bob Kleberg told me, "He was the best cow horse I ever rode, but he was also a damn good running horse. He had that well-balanced look and the feel of a race horse."[4]

Dr. Northway recalled how Bob Kleberg selected the mares for the Old Sorrel's manada. Those that he had not personally ridden were selected on the recommendations of Kineños who had ridden them. If there was still a question about a mare's fitness, Bob Kleberg would have her saddled and ride her himself. When the selection of the original mares was complete, there were browns, blacks, bays, and sorrels in the group. Most showed some Thoroughbred blood, others indicated Spanish origin, and a few were good

---

[3] Denhardt Files, King Ranch Tapes, reel No. 2.

[4] Interview notes, July 11, 1966, Denhardt Files, King Ranch Folder No. 3. Kleberg went on to describe the horse: "Old Sorrel was so good you could not really compare him with other horses, whether you were roping or cutting. This was the type and kind of a horse we wanted. We made up our mind never to lose that blood—to fix that type—so the ranch could produce horses like the Old Sorrel.

"We selected fifty head of using saddle mares, the best we could get from the ranch, as perfectly conformed as possible. Out of the first few colt crops we selected seven stallions, all good performers and good individuals, but not as uniform as we would want eventually. Some were pretty close to the pattern—for example, Peppy and Little Richard. Solis showed too much Thoroughbred. Macanudo probably looked the most like the Old Sorrel, with his long back, and he may have been the best cow horse. However, taking everything into consideration, we selected Solis to breed to his half sisters. The other stallions were used mainly on outcross mares. All our breeding was aimed to produce the conformation and characteristics of the Old Sorrel. One of the best sons of Solis was Wimpy. However, probably the most influential of all of the old Sorrel sons was Hired Hand, who came late. He was like magic after thirty years."

118

Quarter mares. They were purely and simply a cross section of the best using cow-horse mares Bob Kleberg could find on the ranch, with Thoroughbreds predominating. Naturally, no conformation defects, such as crooked legs, ewe necks, or bad heads, were allowed. Although they lacked uniformity, all the mares were top individuals.

Among the first crop of colts that the Old Sorrel begot, three stud colts proved outstanding. They were Little Richard, Tino (described in Chapter 17), and Melon. Both Tino and Melon were gelded, to give two top Old Sorrel colts an opportunity to be real cow horses who didn't have their minds on their manhood. Little Richard was kept entire so that if he proved out he could be returned to the breeding program. Little Richard did indeed turn out extremely well, and was used as the second breeding stallion in the Quarter Horse program—the Old Sorrel, his sire, being the first. Little Richard represented the first of the first-generation stallions. He was used for ten years, from 1927 to 1937.

The Old Sorrel's second crop, born in 1923, produced two more outstanding stud colts. One was Cardenal, and the other was Solis. Both were to have great influence on future horses. Each had a Lazarus Thoroughbred mare for a dam. The rest of the colts were gelded and sent to the ranch remudas. All the fillies were good, but only the top half rejoined their dams in the breeding program.

One outstanding characteristic of the first few crops of colts of the Old Sorrel was their uniformity. Bob Kleberg, Dr. Northway, and Lauro Cavazos have mentioned their amazement at the Old Sorrel's prepotency. The uniformity also extended to the color. Dr. Northway believes that at least 75 per cent of the Old Sorrel's first colts were sorrel, regardless of the color of their dams. The color conformity was proof positive of the Old Sorrel's prepotency and dominance in characteristics.

Some twenty years after the Old Sorrel's first two colt crops were on the ground, Bob Kleberg wrote:

> The first important effort was made when Solis, one of the Old Sorrel's sons out of a Thoroughbred mare, was mated to his daughters from this same band of mares. In the course of a very short time, this band of mares was built up to thirty-five or forty in number, and in this way

119

Solis was mated to forty of his half-sisters, mostly from Thoroughbred mares. The results of this mating were very gratifying, and it was clear that a long stride toward a fixed type had been made in this first mating.

They [the breeders] were fully aware that not every exceptional sire has a balance of genetic qualities which will stand the test of close inbreeding without disaster. The only way in which this could be determined was actual trial. The Old Sorrel was mated on a few occasions to his best daughters, and the results, while encouraging, were not exceptional. But when his son Solis was mated on Old Sorrel daughters, the results were so good that the management decided to try to perpetuate Old Sorrel through line breeding and inbreeding.[5]

There are no complete records of all the Old Sorrel's offspring, of which there were many. Of his progeny fifty-three fillies and fourteen colts were registered.[6] There were ninety-six of his mares in the ranch manadas. How many of the Old Sorrel's stud colts were gelded is also unknown. The Old Sorrel was bred from 1921 to 1943 (he died in 1945). One fact is certain: more than 90 per cent of the cow horses on the ranch are Old Sorrel on both top lines of their pedigree. Since he was in his prime in the 1920's and 1930's, twenty years before the American Quarter Horse Association was organized to maintain pedigree records, we have only the working logs of the ranch and the memories of the old-timers for the early years. The ranch records were adequate for the purposes of the ranch and its divisions. Careful records were kept on the stallions used, with dates and the number of mares. In most cases the mares were not listed as individuals but bore brands showing their breeding, and each colt's record thus showed the sire and the dam's sire. Since each succeeding generation of fillies—all with top lines going to the Old Sorrel—were more and more closely related, no other information was of value to the ranch.

[5] Robert J. Kleberg, Jr. (with A. O. Rhoad), "The Development of a Superior Family in the Quarter Horse," *Journal of Heredity*, August, 1946, 229.

[6] According to Gail Boon, whose job it is to keep the Quarter Horse records for the ranch these figures are questionable. She wrote: "Could only find in our records of mares: 48 registered for the Ranch, 1 sold and registered, 2 not registered for the Ranch, 1 sold and not registered; for stallions, 12 registered for the Ranch (one of the 12 never used as stallion), 5 sold and registered, one not registered for the Ranch, 1 sold and not registered." The list of Old Sorrel offspring in Appendix 8 of this book is taken from the AQHA and other outside sources.

There were exceptions to this practice, as when a superior mare was bought for use as an outcross. Outstanding fillies of such a mare were put back into the mare bands. These outcross mares, such as Water Lilly, were identified, of course. On the whole, however, the mares can be traced back only to a group of closely related sisters, such as Lucky Mose mares or Lazarus mares. The blood is known exactly; the individual mares are unknown.

20. Outcross Stallions—Quarter Horses

$\mathbf{W}$ELL over eighty stallions, none of which were of King Ranch breeding or employed in its Quarter Horse program, appear as the sires of mares used by the ranch in its operations.[1] Most of them were Quarter Horses or Thoroughbreds. The two Quarter Horse bloodlines which made the most important contributions were of Adams or Clegg breeding, for the most part tracing to Rondo or Dan Tucker. Little Joe, Ace of Hearts, Billy Sunday, Cotton Eye (or Cotton Eyed) Joe, Hickory Bill, Little Hickory, Jiggs, and Pancho Villa are examples. The Thoroughbred bloodlines will be discussed in Chapter 21.

It has already been pointed out that when Bob Kleberg started his cow-horse breeding program he added to it any outstanding mare he could buy. That practice accounts for the variegated list of stallions appearing as the sires or grandsires of the Quarter mares in the ranch manadas. As would be expected, some did not produce acceptable conformation and ability, and their female offspring never found their way into the core program. All colts were, of course, gelded and ridden, or sold or given away.

ACE OF HEARTS

Most authorities agree that Little Joe and Rondo were two of the great-

[1] For a list of all stallions appearing in the bloodlines of the King Ranch Quarter Horses, see the Appendices at the end of this book.

est Quarter Horses produced in Texas. Little Joe was to the south country what Peter McCue was to the north. Ace of Hearts was one of the very few horses that managed to beat Little Joe in a race.

When the race was matched, in 1908, it was the talk of the countryside and the biggest event of the year in South Texas. At the time Will Copeland, of Pettus, owned Ace of Hearts, and John Dial was working with him, either because he had an interest in the horse or because he and George Clegg were rivals and he always liked to beat George in a horse race. George had a dream that he was going to lose the race, and he halfway believed his dream. For that reason he was not too badly hurt when his horse came in second, but it broke most of the sports around Alice when Ace came in first. It had been neck and neck all the way. What may have beaten Little Joe was his behavior at the gate. He was nervous and cut up badly, while Ace stood tense but quiet, waiting for the start. As a result, Ace got a jump on Little Joe, something very few horses ever did. That edge proved just enough to give Ace the race.

Ace of Hearts had been bred by Luke Neal, of Gillette, Texas. Ace's dam was Queen, a mare from Louisiana who some claimed had been sired by Dedier. His sire was the Duderstadt Horse, who was by Sykes Rondo. When Ace of Hearts matured, he was fourteen and a half hands high and weighed right at one thousand pounds. He had a white spot on his left side, which gave him his name, and a white right hind foot. When he was six years old, he was sold to Will Copeland. Copeland raced Ace and bred him until the horse's untimely death in 1918. He had been turned out to pasture with his mares and was found with a badly splintered right leg. Though a mare could have caused the injury, it looked more like the result of a stray shot from a deer hunter. Regretfully Copeland had to put Ace out of his misery.

BILLY SUNDAY

The ranch had only two Billy Sunday mares. Billy was somewhat coarse, but he had royal blood. He was incorrectly registered as a Thoroughbred, under the name Huyler. Billy, a sorrel, was born in 1916. He was sired by the Thoroughbred Horace H and out of Carrie Nation. He was bred by John Wilkins, of San Antonio. In 1917 he was purchased by J. E. Parke, of Kyle,

123

Texas. Later some fancy horse trading took place. Ott Adams owned Jim Wells, who was by Little Joe. Jim Wells went from Ott Adams to John Dial to Graves Peeler to John E. Parke. Billy Sunday reversed that route, going from Parke to Peeler to Adams.

Billy Sunday had been registered so that he could run on the organized tracks. His dam was the great mare Carrie Nation, a world record holder for the five-eighths mile. Carrie was also registered in the Jockey Club as Belle of Oakford. In a letter to Ott Adams dated December 17, 1919, John Wilkins wrote that Billy Sunday's dam, Belle of Oakford, was nicknamed Carrie Nation. Carrie had been bred by Samuel Watkins in Illinois and was sired by Peter McCue, and thus was a half sister of Hickory Bill.

COTTON EYE JOE

Cotton Eye Joe was a bald-faced sorrel horse with one glass eye. He had a lot of roan hairs in his flanks and at the root of his tail. Both of his hind feet were also white. He was a heavily quartered, good-looking horse weighing about 1,050 pounds and standing fourteen–two and a half hands. He was by Little Joe and out of Little Sister by Little Joe. He was bred and raised by Ott Adams.

George Clegg bought Cotton Eye Joe from Adams and raced him successfully for several years. He then sold him to Tom East, of the King Ranch, who bred him for a while. The ranch did not like the glass eye or the extra white which appeared in most of his offspring. The white was too susceptible to sandburn. In 1932, Cotton Eye Joe was traded to the Waggoners, of Vernon, Texas, for a Yellow Jacket colt. The Waggoners used Cotton Eye Joe until 1935 or 1936. Any mares that the King Ranch owned that show Yellow Jack as the sire were sired by the Yellow Jacket for whom they exchanged Cotton Eye Joe.

JOE ABB

Joe Abb and Joe Moore also furnished some mares to the ranch. Both stallions were raised by Adams. Joe Abb was by Little Joe and out of Genevieve. He was also known as the Strickland Horse. He was foaled in 1923 and was a beautiful sorrel, standing just a little over fourteen–two hands. He

124

was owned at one time or another by most of the South Texas Quarter Horse breeders. Adams first gave Joe Abb to Dr. Strickland in payment for a doctor bill. Others who owned him were Antonio Perez, John Almond, Tom East, Alonzo Taylor, O. W. Cardwell, R. C. Tatum, and E. A. Showers.

JOE MOORE

Joe Moore was the stallion Adams chose to take the place of Little Joe. He was sired by Little Joe and out of the famous Della Moore. He was foaled in 1927. He was a bay, was a bit long-bodied, and stood a scant fourteen hands. Adams owned him all his life, and he proved to be a real sire. The ranch also had some mares by Pancho Villa, who was a son of Little Joe and out of Jeanette.

JIGGS

In its breeding program the ranch had several mares by Jiggs, a sorrel foaled in 1924. Although he had many characteristics of a Thoroughbred, Jiggs was not a purebred. He was sired by Uncle Jimmy Gray, the outstanding Thoroughbred Remount Service stallion that stood in San Antonio. Jimmy was by Bonnie Joe by Faustus. Jiggs's first dam was also a Thoroughbred, but his second dam was a Quarter mare by Sykes Rondo. Jiggs was bred by E. E. Wisdom, of San Antonio. He passed through several hands and was finally purchased by Richard Kleberg, Sr. When the ranch was through with Jiggs, he was given to George Clegg. George used Jiggs for a while and then sold him to Fred Barnett, of Comstock, Texas. Jiggs produced some excellent rodeo horses.

LITTLE HICKORY

The story of Hickory Bill has been related in Chapter 16. Little Hickory, who also furnished some mares, was by Hickory Bill and out of Mary Bell by John Gardner. Little Hickory was a full brother of Albert, the Rooke horse. When he was a yearling, Clegg gave him to the King Ranch, where he was bred to a few mares. Eleven of his fillies were put into the Quarter Horse breeding program.

125

SPOKANE

In January, 1945, Raymond Dickson sold Bob Kleberg eight mares. Five of them were by Dr. Rose, one was by Lobo, and two were by My Pardner. Six were out of Spokane mares. Spokane was by Paul El, who was by Hickory Bill. Paul El, who was out of Baby Ruth, was foaled in 1914 and died in 1940. He too was owned by several well-known breeders, including Ott Adams and John Dial. The ranch had four Paul El mares.

SAM WATKINS

Sam Watkins, foaled in 1913, was also a Hickory Bill colt, and is sometimes referred to as the Clegg Cut Foot Horse. He was out of Hattie W. by Hi Henry. He was a good-looking bay horse. The King Ranch bred him for one year, calling him the Clegg Cut Foot Horse.

TEXAS STAR

Texas Star, who also furnished some blood to the King Ranch, was related to Sam Watkins. Texas Star was bred by George Clegg and was foaled in 1935. He was by Lone Star by Billy Sunday and out of a Sam Watkins mare.

A few other outside stallions who furnished fillies for the King Ranch program are discussed elsewhere in this book.

21. Outcross Stallions—Thoroughbreds

OVER the years stallions had been purchased by the King Ranch as needed. Many were Thoroughbreds. As a result a large number of the ranch mares were also Thoroughbreds. Registration was not important to the ranch, since the offspring were intended solely for ranch use. Once a horse had proved satisfactory, there was no attempt to keep detailed pedigrees. In the cow-horse program manadas were designated by stallions. The manager of any division always knew which horses were from which manada. His reports gave the sire and the dam's sire. That is why parentage is known specifically for any group but not for individuals. Neither the Quarter Horse nor the Thoroughbred registration and breeding program was well established until the 1920's and 1930's.

An example in point is the Thoroughbred San Vicente, who lived in the early 1900's and who appears in the pedigrees of some of the best ranch mares. Only two facts are well known. His parents came from manadas of purebred Thoroughbreds. His brand showed him to be by either Old Tom, a purebred Thoroughbred, or Young Tom, his purebred son. He was foaled on the Laureles Division. According to Dr. Northway, Laureles had top horses and mares. They were somewhat larger than the Santa Gertrudis horses, standing on a little more leg and showing their Thoroughbred parentage to a greater extent.

In those days the horses from the different divisions of the ranch were

127

more stabilized. They were not moved around very much. In later years, with the arrival of trucks and improved roads, the ranch started moving cow outfits from one division to another as they were needed. Dr. Northway described the differences in the horses on the various divisions:

> . . . there was a very definite horse family located on the Laureles Division. This family was called the Frenton Family, which, translated into English, means a rather bulging type of forehead. You probably recall the painting which hung in the library at the Main Residence of two of the former Latin American foremen who were tops and very good men—the best of their profession. One was Euvence García, Sr., foreman of the Norias Division, mounted on his top horse. The other was Augustín Quintanilla, who was mounted on his horse, a top cutting horse named Frenton. That painting shows very definitely the bulging-forehead characteristics of this family. We spoke of them and named them the Frenton Family.[1]

Thoroughbred mares were regularly bred to the Old Sorrel, particularly in the early years, when the Lazarus Thoroughbred blood provided the original basis for the program. Though the Lazarus mares had not been bred especially for use in the cow-horse program, they happened to be strong in the characteristics Bob Kleberg was seeking. One of the Lazarus mares had a colt by Right Royal (TB), who was named Martins Best. He was trained as a cow horse by Bob Kleberg. Later, when Martins Best fillies were introduced into the program, they proved his blood to be one of the most important among the Thoroughbreds used.

After the first few years, Thoroughbred blood was generally introduced only by breeding a Quarter mare from the program to a Thoroughbred stallion having desirable characteristics. The half-bred filly was then introduced into the breeding manada. No matter which way the blood was obtained—by purebred mares or by half-bred mares—the horse colts were eliminated and the fillies were tested before they were put into the brood-mare bands. It is interesting to note that, although other mares were occasionally found in the Quarter Horse mare bands, only those horses tracing

---

[1] Letter from Dr. Northway dated February 14, 1968, Denhardt Files, Northway Folder.

128

directly to the Old Sorrel were in the core program. All others were tempo-rary boarders being bred to one of the program stallions.

All purebred King Ranch Quarter Horses today trace both their top lines to the Old Sorrel. Some trace many lines to the old horse. For ex-ample, Laurel K (AQHA 7338) was by Peppy Jr. and out of Redoma de Laureles. Peppy Jr. was by Peppy, who was a grandson of the Old Sorrel. Peppy Jr.'s dam was Gabriela 2d by Solis, who was by the Old Sorrel. Laurel K's dam, Redoma de Laureles, was by Tomate Laureles by the Old Sorrel, and her dam was Queen Chiquita by Little Richard by the Old Sorrel. In other words the top line of all four grandparents of Laurel K trace to the Old Sorrel, as well as the top line of one of the great-granddams. This is why Bob Kleberg has been so successful first in perpetuating the desirable qual-ities of the Old Sorrel and second in adding some Thoroughbred character-istics without losing those of the Quarter Horse. He has never allowed Thor-oughbred blood to dominate the Old Sorrel but has used it with restraint and only to offset some specific conformation inadequacy.

MARTINS BEST

When the original decision was made to reproduce the abilities possessed by the Old Sorrel, an immediate search was made to find adequate mares on the ranch. If one were to pick a single Thoroughbred stallion who has done more than any other Thoroughbred for the King Ranch Quarter Horses, it would have to be Chicaro. One could also make a good case for Martins Best, however, and he deserves first mention.

Martins Best, foaled in 1909, was raised on the ranch. According to his pedigree, he was sired by Right Royal and out of Grief. Martins Best was a bay horse. His sire, Right Royal, was a grandson of Bend Or and St. Simon. His dam, Grief, was a daughter of Faustus by Inquirer by *Leamington and out of Belle Broeck by Ten Broeck.

The daughters of Martins Best were lumped into the general category of Lazarus mares. They comprised a sizable group of the original mare band given to the Old Sorrel. The Lazarus horses were small for Thoroughbreds, carried a lot of refinement, and had good mouths. Bob Kleberg says that the Old Sorrel's daughters by the Lazarus mares were among the best mares

129

bred on the ranch.[2] This group includes Anita Castilla, Liebra, Motes Brisa, and Toalla. The mares, crossed on the Old Sorrel, were responsible for the best of the Old Sorrel's first sons. The Lazarus stock produced Little Richard, Cardenal, Solis, and Charro. They in turn furnished the dams and grand-dams of many of the other Quarter Horse sires. It was only with the introduction of Little Joe blood, which came a bit later, that mares equal to the Lazarus brood mares were produced.

CHICARO

It was the decision to buy some Little Joe mares for the program that brought Bob Kleberg face to face with Chicaro for the first time. In 1934 he went to Goliad to try to buy Ada Jones. At the time she was owned by John Dial. Kleberg bought her and several other mares. As he was about to leave, Dial asked him whether he would like to see a pretty good Thoroughbred he had picked up during a recent trip to New Orleans. Dial explained that the horse, a Whitney-bred colt, had not been raced and had been neglected by his owner.[3] In fact, he had almost died of pneumonia. Dial was an expert horseman, and he knew what a stallion the horse would prove to be when he had filled out. John Dial had the South Texan's affinity for compact musculature in a horse, and in Chicaro, as the horse was named, he saw a sire of great potential value for his area. Dial made discreet inquiries about the neglected stallion and learned his breeding and history. He liked what he heard and bought the horse in 1928. He took Chicaro home to Goliad and began to pour the feed to him and groomed him regularly. (Incidentally, on the trip home Dial stopped a night in Abbeville, Louisiana. During the stopover Chicaro was bred to Zerengue's Belle, who in due time foaled the famous Flying Bob.)

When Bob Kleberg saw Chicaro at John Dial's ranch, he realized here was a stallion that had almost all the Thoroughbred characteristics he wanted

2 Bob Kleberg said of Martins Best: "The daughter of this horse and some of his inbred daughters were the best mares that were bred to the Old Sorrel." Memo dated June 24, 1960, Denhardt Files, King Ranch Folder No. 4.

3 "I do not think Chicaro ever got to race. The story is that he pawed a plank off a fence sticking a nail through his ankle and he was crippled for a long time." Letter from Bob Kleberg dated May 20, 1969, Denhardt Files, King Ranch Folder No. 3.

to obtain for his cow horses. Chicaro was strong where Quarter Horses were weak. He was refined, with a beautiful back and withers and good shoulders. He was not leggy, but rather compact and very heavily muscled, like a Quarter Horse. In short, he had in abundance those characteristics often lacking in the South Texas Quarter Horses. Kleberg bought Chicaro in 1934 for four thousand dollars, and took him home to the Santa Gertrudis, along with Ada Jones and the other mares he had come to purchase.

Chicaro was not the first Thoroughbred the ranch had bought, but he had class and quality lacking in earlier purchases. Chicaro's sire was imported *Chicle by Spearmint and out of Lady Hamburg. Chicaro's dam was bred even better. She was Wendy, a sister of Elf, the dam of Boojum, a speed merchant. Wendy was by Peter Pan, a grandson of Domino and out of Remembrance. Remembrance was also the dam of Bonus, whose son was Twenty Grand. Perhaps Wendy bore more responsibility for Chicaro's heavily muscled conformation than *Chicle.

Chicaro's arrival caused Bob Kleberg to begin studying Thoroughbred bloodlines. Until that time he had been interested primarily in conformation and action. Perhaps, he thought, blood was the key to improving the Old Sorrel Quarter Horses. His study of Thoroughbred bloodlines was later to stand Kleberg in good stead when he began breeding Thoroughbreds to race. By the time he had decided to enter this demanding game he already knew more about the top Thoroughbred bloodlines than all but half a dozen Thoroughbred scholars, most of whom were not practicing breeders.

Chicaro proved very successful in providing outcross blood for the Quarter Horse program. About twenty mares sired by Chicaro were thus used. They included La Billetera, Cambiada, Chicara, Chicaro's Hallie, Chicharita Segunda, Chic Tex Pride, Delicatesa de Texas (Texas Pride), Esperanza, Huerfanita de Chicaro, Lucy Brown, Matera de Chicaro, Milky Way, La Mindieta, Mrs. S., Petrita, Villitera, and others. Cambiada was out of Ada Jones and was a full sister of the stallion John Dial. She was also the dam of Boiler Maker. Chicara was out of an Ace of Hearts mare and was the dam of Winny de Beto, dam of King Hand. Chicaro's Hallie was the dam of Bruja. Bruja was the dam of Miss Princess (Woven Web) and of Mickie (Witchbrew). Texas Pride was the dam of Maggie (Chovasco).

131

Chicharita was out of a Solis mare and was one of the best mares on the ranch. Chic Tex Pride was out of Water Lilly, as was Delicatesa de Texas.

A Thoroughbred son of Chicaro, Sudden Change, was also used by the ranch as a sire for outcross mares. Sudden Change was bred by John Dial. His dam was Prides Ella. He sired twelve mares: Adelita, Bernice, La Brava, China Poblana, Dorado Cola Delgada, Escura Gatcha, Fidelita, Oscura Gacha, Pluma, Rabona Encino, Sorda, and one unnamed daughter. John Dial, another son, was also used sparingly.

BIM BAM AND BOLD VENTURE

Two stallions sired by *St. Germans, Bim Bam and Bold Venture, also contributed to the ranch program. Bim Bam's dam was Elf by *Chicle, and Bold Venture's dam was Possible by Ultimus. Mares introduced into the program by Bim Bam were Estufa and Overwhelming. The Bold Venture females were Border Venture and Madam Queen. The famous Quarter running mare Miss Princess (Woven Web) was sired by Bold Venture and out of Bruja. Bold Venture's son, Depth Charge, sired several fillies used in the program. Depth Charge was out of Quickly by Haste. Mares by Depth Charge were Bon Bec, Lantana Queen, Reticule, Silva's Brown, and Touching.

Another speedy Thoroughbred, Boojum, was also used to some extent. Boojum was by John P. Grier and out of Elf by *Chicle. Bruja II and Cactus Hallie were the mares sired by Boojum that were used in the program. Boojum was also the sire of the fast-running Quarter Horse Nobody's Friend, who was out of Pal by Alamo. One mare by the great Equestrian (Equipoise-Frilette) was used—a filly named Occlusion.

REMOUNT HORSES

As has been mentioned elsewhere, several Army Remount Service stallions sired mares used by the ranch in its Quarter Horse program. Lion D'Or, discussed elsewhere, contributed three mares. Another Remount stallion, Rex Beach II, was used by George Clegg, and some of his blood was used. Rex Beach II was sired by Rex Beach. He was foaled in 1912, a brown horse bred by O. G. Parke, of Kyle, Texas. His sire was Conjurar, and his dam was Teo Beach, who was out of Mamie J by Little Joe.

132

There were three horses called Naughty Boy. The original horse of that name was imported *Naughty Boy II, an English Thoroughbred purchased by the Army Remount Service. He was used by Anastachio Saenz, in Jim Wells County. *Naughty Boy II was by Lemonora by Lemberg and out of Mademoiselle by Oppressor. Naughty Boy III was a beautiful chestnut stallion, a little on the leggy side. He was by *Naughty Boy II and out of Toalla by Martins Best. Mrs. Bob Kleberg liked him and used him to breed hunters and jumpers. She selected some Old Sorrel fillies that were a little on the leggy side and bred Naughty Boy III to them. Some of the fillies produce eventually found their way back into the brood-mare band, among them Botella and La Tachita. Naughty Boy I was also sired by *Naughty Boy II. He was out of a Solis mare, and the ranch used two of his daughters in the program.

The other Remount Service horse was Lovely Manners. He was by Sweep and out of *Sournoise. The ranch used five mares by Lovely Manners, three of whom were China Chiquita, Remendada, and Virginia Dare. Another well-known son of Lovely Manners was Don Manners, discussed at some length elsewhere.

REMOLINO

The only other Thoroughbred stallion important enough to be mentioned here is Remolino. He represents the Ariel line, a strain noted for its early speed, which is also a Quarter Horse characteristic. Remolino was by Ariel and out of Flying Dust by High Cloud by Ultimus. Several fillies by Remolino were used in the program: American Girl, Chovasca, Cola Delgado, Oscuva de Encino, Prieta Panda, Remolina, and Samuela. Remolino's greatest contributions to the Quarter Horse program came when he was crossed on Solis mares. Those individuals had just about everything. When Remolino was bred to Bruja, he sired Mickie (Witchbrew); and when he was bred to Texas Pride, he sired Maggie (Chovasco). Both of these mares burned up the short tracks from Arizona to Louisiana. They were raced by Ernest Lane.

22. First-Generation Stallions

WHEN the first mares had been selected to be bred to the old Sorrel, there was nothing to do but wait. To Bob Kleburg and his cohorts spring seem a long time coming.

When the foals finally began to arrive, they looked good—very good. It appeared that the Old Sorrel had put a group of worthy sons and daughters on the ground. It was now necessary to wait three or four more years to see whether they could perform as well as they looked. A few mares whose progeny did not seem quite up to snuff were taken out of the Old Sorrel's manada and replaced by other good mares. So time passed.

Extra care was used to select colts that were to be used as stallions in the breeding program. A mare could make one mistake a year; a stallion used in error could be many times more costly. The fact that the horses would be bred back to some close relatives made the importance of straight legs, good heads, and proper temperament just that much more important. When all of the first crop of colts had been ridden, only one was selected to join the Old Sorrel in the program. His name was Little Richard.

Little Richard

Little Richard was foaled in 1922. He was a beautiful sorrel, and his dam was a ranch mare, sired by the Thoroughbred Lucky Mose. Little Richard was selected only after he had been ridden in competition with his half

134

brothers. Not until a consensus of the ranch employees was reached was he finally chosen by Bob Kleberg as the first new stallion added to the program. Several individuals were in on the judging in those early days. Caesar Kleberg and Sam Ragland were often consulted, as was Richard Kleberg, when he was available. Much of the advisory work fell on the capable shoulders of Lauro Cavazos, the ranch foreman; Dr. Northway, the ranch veterinarian; and the division bosses: Ed Durham, of Norias; Charley Burwell, of Laureles; and Jim McBride, of Encino. The Kineños who did most of the riding were also consulted. They compared notes on the various horses, and then Bob Kleberg made the final decision. The first big one was to select Little Richard as the number-two stallion.

Little Richard was used from 1927 to 1937. The ranch work sheets show that eighteen fillies and one colt sired by him were registered in the American Quarter Horse Association. Seventy of his daughters were returned to the breeding program. Only one son followed him into the breeding program—Peppy, one of the outstanding second-generation stallions. The reason that no more of his offspring were registered is that the ranch used hundreds of horses in its cow-horse operations and many more in the specialized Quarter Horse project. Only those individuals considered outstanding were submitted for registration with the American Quarter Horse Association, and not all of those entered the core program. It must also be remembered that the ranch was breeding only for its own use. Even in later years, when the demand required a yearly sale, the breeding program was maintained because it furnished cow horses for the ranch, not because a sale was in the offing.

CARDENAL AND SOLIS

The next year's colt crop, the second, arrived in the spring of 1923. From this group of foals two stallions, Cardenal and Solis, were worked under the saddle and selected for the program. All the others were gelded and used as cow horses. Cardenal was out of a Lazarus mare who was by Right Royal. Cardenal was used from 1928 to 1935. None of his sons were kept as stallions. Eight of his fillies were eventually registered, and fifty-six were used in the breeding program.

135

Solis, the second stallion saved from the 1923 crop, was ridden and tested until 1929. Like Cardenal, he was out of a Lazarus mare. In bloodline both he and Cardenal were approximately seven-eighths Thoroughbred and one-eighth Quarter Horse.[1] Fifty-four of Solis' daughters and two of his colts were registered. Altogether ninety mares by Solis were used in the breeding program, and four of his sons saw service in the stud.

TOMATE LAURELES

Tomate Laureles was the next son of the Old Sorrel to be kept as a stallion and used in the program. He was foaled in 1927, one of the sixth crop. His dam was a crack Quarter mare, the one referred to as the Dock Lawrence Mare (her story is found in Chapter 18). Tomate Laureles was the first stallion with a predominance of Quarter Horse blood; he was five-eighths Quarter Horse and three-eighths Thoroughbred. His dam was sired by Tom Thumb, who was by Little Joe, and she was out of a daughter of Hickory Bill. Tomate was used in the ranch breeding program from 1929 to 1949 and was unexcelled as a producer of female stock. Fifty-one of his fillies were used by the ranch, seventeen of his colts were gelded and ridden by the Kineños, and four were left stallions and sold. None of his stallions were used in the program.

BABE GRANDE

From the colt crop for the next year, 1928, only one stud colt was kept entire and used as a stallion in the program. His name was Babe Grande. He too was a well-bred Quarter Horse like Tomate Laureles, having five eighths Quarter Horse and three-eighths Thoroughbred blood in his veins. He was also noted for the excellence of his brood mares. Possibly he was a little hard on the bit, but his natural cow sense was so absolute that it made his other slight imperfections seem unimportant. His ability to transmit his cow sense was fortunately recognized early, and he was used from 1931 to 1951. He sired ninety-three registered fillies and eighty-two unregistered ones. He sired 112 horse colts, fifteen of which were registered. None of his colts were returned to the breeding band because of the imperfections

[1] See Appendix 1, List 3, at the end of this book.

noted above. He made his contribution through the blood of his mares. Of his mares, 109 were placed in the Quarter Horse brood bands. The other mares and geldings were ridden by the Kineños.

TINO

Bob Kleberg's favorite riding mare produced the next stallion kept in the program. Foaled in 1932, the stallion, like his earlier brothers, was named Tino. His dam was Brisa, a Thoroughbred mare sired by San Vicente and out of a purebred, though unregistered, Thoroughbred ranch mare. Tino was used from 1934 to 1948, and sired forty-nine fillies that were registered and kept by the ranch and thirty-eight others that were used but not registered. Thirty-nine of his colts were gelded and ridden. Fifty-one of his mares were returned to the breeding program, the others being ridden by the Kineños. More about his dam, Brisa, is found in Chapter 17.

CHARRO

The next year Charro was selected. Charro was out of Toalla, who was by the Thoroughbred Martins Best. In bloodline he was, like Little Richard, Solis, Cardenal, and Tino, seven-eighths Thoroughbred and one-eighth Quarter Horse. Like his half brothers, however, he was more Quarter Horse than Thoroughbred in conformation. (All his progeny, both filly and colt, that showed too much Thoroughbred were taken out of the program.) Charro was used from 1936 to 1941 and sired ten fillies and three colts. Soon afterward he was sold to the Remount Service of the Peruvian army. In Peru he sired many sons and daughters who are still in use.

MACANUDO

Macanudo, from the 1934 foal crop, was the next stallion selected for the program. Macanudo probably looked the most like the Old Sorrel, long back and all. He was also the best cow horse of the first generation. Macanudo was out of Canales Bell, one of the three Quarter mares that were the dams of first-generation sires. Macanudo was used from 1937 to 1949. Among his get were 145 fillies, 65 registered and 80 unregistered. The ranch kept 128 and sold 17. Macanudo had 110 colts, 21 registered and 89 un-

137

registered. The ranch gelded 76 and kept 3 stallions. The rest were sold. Of his fillies, 71 were put back into the program, and 2 of his colts, Dos de Oros and Chamaco, were used. His blood was very nearly 50 per cent Quarter Horse and 50 per cent Thoroughbred.

LITTLE MAN

The next important stallion was Little Man. Little Man was out of Water Lilly, the best breeding Quarter mare the King Ranch owned. He was foaled in 1941 and was used from 1944 to 1955. During that time 28 of his fillies and 8 of his colts were registered. In all, he sired 62 fillies and 64 colts. He would have had many more, but he was a shy breeder. He was probably as good an individual as his brother, Hired Hand.

TEJANO

One of the last sons of the Old Sorrel to be used by the ranch was Tejano. He was out of the mare Delicatesa de Texas, who was out of Water Lilly and by Chicaro. Tejano was foaled in 1942 and was used from 1945 to 1956. He produced 100 fillies and 79 colts. None of his sons were used by the ranch, but 25 of his fillies were placed in the manadas.

HIRED HAND

Hired Hand, foaled in 1943, was the Old Sorrel's last, and greatest, son used on the ranch. He too was the product of Water Lilly. The King Ranch registered 172 of his fillies and 60 of his colts. Of his mares, 54 were used in the breeding program, and of his sons 7 were used as Quarter Horse stallions by the ranch. Others found their way into outside hands through sales and gifts. An indication of his prepotency is the fact that he has 11 grandsons and 3 great-grandsons in use as stallions on the ranch. No other sire of the first generation even comes close to this record. His sons are King Hand, El Shelton, El Perfumo, El Nino, Hired Hand's Cardinal (also spelled Cardenal), Tipo de Norias, and Hired Hand II. His grandsons are Cardenal Chico, El Alejos, Gonzalo Cardenal, El Brooks, Jardinero Red, Reganio, El Moral, Venadito, Algo, El Columpio, and Mr. Kleberg. His great-grandsons are Mendigo, Senor Dulce, and El Vaiven.

138

When the Old Sorrel died in 1945, his great son, Hired Hand, took his place. He was produced when the Old Sorrel was thirty years old. Since Hired Hand was the Old Sorrel's best son, he provided an opportunity to return to the fountainhead of the breed. Hired Hand was used on the tail male descendants of the Old Sorrel many removes from the old horse. A plan was formulated to use Hired Hand's sons extensively to fix type and quality. This step probably did more for the uniformity, quality, and type of the King Ranch Quarter Horse than any other single decision made after 1912, when the Old Sorrel was purchased and the program started.

SMOKY

As a sort of footnote, a few other stallions sired by the Old Sorrel proved important, though they had no appreciable influence on the breeding program. For example, there was Smoky, a grullo horse foaled in 1934. He was by the Old Sorrel and out of La Ruben. He was used on a handful of ranch mares but spent most of his life on the Hebbronville Ranch with Tom East. Another of the Old Sorrel's sons was Old Man, foaled in 1935 and sold as a yearling to Volney Hildreth, of Aledo, Texas. He was out of one of Cardenal's daughters. He was never used by the ranch.

COMANCHE

Another stallion, of somewhat different type and color, was Comanche. He was dun in color but was an exceptional individual. Consequently, like Smoky, he was retained by the ranch but was bred only on another division. Comanche was bred on Norias and at Encino and did not enter the key Quarter Horse program. His dam was the Pyle Dun Mare. In his later years he was sold into Mexico.

BOILER MAKER

Boiler Maker, another son by the Old Sorrel, was out of a daughter of Ada Jones named Cambiada. He was foaled in 1942 and was loaned to Albert George, of Richmond, Texas. He was returned to the ranch after a number of years and was bred briefly and then given to a friend of Bob Kleberg's, Don Stone, who ranched in Oklahoma and in the Río Grande Valley.

23. The Breeding Program

Serious breeding has but one purpose—the improvement of the breed. It is an attempt to produce animals that will fulfill man's requirements a little better. Until the 1920's, when the internal-combustion engine replaced horses and mules on the roads, horse breeding was generally one of "breeding up." That was true on the King Ranch as it was on all other ranches. Except on a few purebred farms, draft and carriage horses were raised by putting purebred stallions on grade mares. Saddle animals were upgraded by the use of Remount Service stallions or other desirable light horses. After tractors, trucks, and passenger cars replaced draft horses, dray horses, and saddle horses, the emphasis in breeding changed from high-grades to purebreds. Horses raised primarily as a hobby must be selected individuals, and purebreds are better than crossbreds.

Even such large and well-known ranches as the King Ranch must have good purebred animals or informed buyers who are ready to spend money will not be attracted to their sales. Sales of surplus or unwanted individuals provide additional revenue with little extra expense when horses must be raised in any case. The intelligent ranchers gained by the demand for purebreds. They could now emphasize certain family characteristics or concentrate on certain superior individuals. It was the above factors that made the King Ranch horses so popular.

Breeding horses is not quite as simple as breeding good beef cattle or

140

dairy cattle. In the latter one is breeding for a known, concrete factor: beef or butterfat. In breeding horses one is trying to produce a less tangible quality: performance that springs from ability and desire. All breeders know that performance is closely tied to type and general conformation. It is the next step that separates the real breeder from one who merely breeds horses. The gifted breeder aims not just for type and conformation but also for action, temperament, and endurance, since those are the qualities that determine superior performance. It is clear that breeding for a quality such as desire or temperament is not a simple matter, especially when that quality must be accompanied by ability to perform.

A horse's disposition, or temperament, is an essential ingredient for performance. The need for it is equal to, and may even exceed, that for conformation. *Disposition* represents the "ability to learn" the tasks for which a horse may be trained and the "desire to execute," or perform, those tasks when called on. *Endurance* is the ability to work when tired, to give that little extra effort when called upon. *Action* is the freedom of movement that makes the task easier to accomplish.

The pedigree can be a clue to an individual's temperament, and conformation indicates whether the individual can perform if he desires to do so. Horses with poor conformation sometimes have the heart and will to perform, while beautifully conformed individuals may be sloppy in action or too lazy to move fast. Beef from lazy cows may taste as good as that from vigorous ones, but performance and action in a horse are nothing without the right temperament and desire.

The reader who has progressed this far in the book has gained some idea of Bob Kleberg's method of meeting this challenge in his breeding program. Kleberg had great personal ability as a geneticist and breeder. He also had some advantages of a supplementary nature that were a big help to him: he had excellent men, and he was working with a sufficient number of animals that he was able to select and eliminate. Perhaps a certain amount of luck was involved in finding the Old Sorrel, but he *was* found, and he *was* put to use. A great deal of credit for the success of the program was due to the early realization of the potential of the Old Sorrel. Too often great sires are not recognized until after they are gone.

141

During the first twenty-five to thirty years of the program, Bob Kleberg personally supervised the breeding, making every major decision and guiding the directions of all lesser ones. Then, as ranch business expanded, more and more of the day-to-day direction of the ranch activities were turned over to Richard M. Kleberg, Jr., Bob Kleberg's nephew. Since 1940, Dick Kleberg, who has the Kleberg eye for cattle and horses, has been, with his uncle's advice and help, the prime factor in the continued development of the ranch Quarter Horses.

Most of the early daughters of the Old Sorrel were bred to Solis, who came from the same band of mares. This practice ensured concentration and preservation not only of the conformation but also of the ability of the Old Sorrel. As a safety factor, and to provide outcross blood, many outstanding Quarter mares were purchased. They were introduced into the program and bred to the Old Sorrel, his sons, grandsons, and so on.

Selections were made from the saddle-tested offspring in such a fashion as to mate those individuals that would complement each other. Care was taken never to double up weaknesses but always to double on strength. The model or pattern was always the Old Sorrel. Little Richard, for example, was a little bigger than the Old Sorrel. Cardenal was a bit smaller. So Cardenal fillies were bred to Little Richard, and vice versa. In this fashion each animal was bred to fit the pattern of the Old Sorrel.

Originally it had been hoped that the Old Sorrel would prove prepotent enough to breed to his own daughters without recessive defects in the offspring. He was bred to several of his daughters, and they were not exceptional. Bob Kleberg then decided to perpetuate the Old Sorrel by line breeding.[1] Tested fillies were bred back and forth among the sons of the Old Sorrel, each mating being designed to supplement and concentrate characteristics.

When Hired Hand proved himself to be, as Bob Kleberg said, "like magic after thirty years," Bob and Dick Kleberg had an important decision to make. Should the program go on disseminating the blood of the Old Sorrel through the use of a number of his sons, or should the program once more be concentrated in an effort to achieve uniformity of type and character by

[1] "Development of a Superior Family of the Quarter Horse," *Journal of Heredity,* Vol. XXXVII (August, 1946), 233.

focusing the program on the genes of his best son, Hired Hand? The decision was made in favor of Hired Hand; the results have more than equaled expectations. As before, other sons and outcross blood are kept available, all-top-line descendants of the Old Sorrel.

The closeness of breeding practiced by the King Ranch can be seen from the following statistics. The inbreeding coefficient of the Quarter Horse breed as a whole is an average of 1.2 per cent. The two thousand Quarter Horses in the King Ranch program have an average inbreeding of 8.6 per cent.[2] It is interesting to examine the blood of some of the better-known King Ranch stallions. Wimpy was a double grandson of the Old Sorrel. Both Wimpy and the mares to whom he was bred carried at least one half the blood of the Old Sorrel, but, since they had different dams, they were only 25 per cent related to each other. Wimpy's offspring from the Old Sorrel mares were 62.5 per cent related to the Old Sorrel. That is an increase of 12.5 per cent over that of their parents.

The mares to whom Wimpy was bred averaged 60.3 per cent Quarter Horse and 39.7 per cent Thoroughbred. The mating scheme used gave his offspring 67.7 per cent Quarter Horse, an increase from 60.3 per cent of their dams. Most of the increase was the result of concentrating the blood of the Old Sorrel, whose genes in the offspring increased from 39.7 to 44.9 per cent.

In the case of Macanudo and Babe Grande the Thoroughbred genes were reduced even more, since each had a Quarter mare dam. In Macanudo the Thoroughbred genes dropped from 55 per cent in the dams to 27.4 per cent in his foals. Babe Grande's foals represented a drop in Thoroughbred genes from 43.5 per cent in the dams to 18.1 per cent in the offspring.[3]

The above data indicate a fair amount of inbreeding. Yet Bob Kleberg did not inbreed the Quarter Horses as much as he did the Santa Gertrudis cattle. The uncertain factors represented by the terms *temperament*, *action*, and *endurance* made all-out inbreeding in horses too dangerous. His plan was to maintain a relationship to the Old Sorrel but to skip a generation by

[2] See *Annual Sale Catalog, King Ranch*, April 18, 1968, 18–19.
[3] "Development of a Superior Family of the Quarter Horse," *Journal of Heredity*, Vol. XXXVIII (August, 1946), 235.

mating uncles to nieces, not fathers to daughters. Outcrosses were made with some regularity as a control factor, since line breeding can be a two-edged sword.

Line breeding concentrates good qualities, but by the same token it can also magnify bad qualities. The outcross mares made available fillies with enough new blood to halt the spread of any deleterious tendencies in the breeding bands. Since the blood of the Old Sorrel—and lately the blood of Hired Hand—was being concentrated, special care and attention were taken to be sure that the fillies did not take on masculine characteristics. Another factor that could give trouble, one that crops out in many inbred animals, was the loss of libido, or vigor and fertility. Here again the outcross females provided a safety factor. Care was also taken to eliminate from the breeding program any horse that showed an indication of such defects.

At King Ranch the breeding program is carried on in a manner similar to that of most other well-operated ranches. The stallion is introduced to his mares in a ten- to fifteen-acre paddock. After getting acquainted with them for about twenty-four hours, he accepts them, and during the first week in March they are all turned out into a larger pasture. There the stallion settles on a certain range and keeps his mares in that general area. From that time he will not take in any other mares, nor will he allow any of his manada to stray off.

The number of mares allotted to each stallion is determined by a number of factors, although a stallion is seldom turned out with fewer than twenty or more than thirty-five or forty mares. The stallions are generally brought back to their paddock around the middle of June.[4]

When branding time comes in the fall, the manadas are brought in and the colts are led out individually for inspection and criticism. In the beginning Bob Kleberg made the decisions, but now Dick Kleberg has this responsibility. All colts are graded Top, Good to Top, Good, Fair to Good, Fair, No Good. On the record of each colt is also marked such qualities as stud prospect, light-boned, sale prospect, overshot, crooked hocks, brands, bad head, enlarged naval, and so on. Only the two top grades are put through

4 Detailed information on this procedure may be found in Appendix 5 at the end of this book.

144

the tests required of those who may be used in the breeding program. The rest are put in the remudas for work on the ranch or are sold.

As has been pointed out earlier, each sire and dam used in the program is tested under saddle and is not used unless he or she quickly gains the proficiency required of the breeding stock. As each succeeding generation has come and gone over almost half a century, the ranch has only made a handful of exceptions to this rule, and most of them were chosen as outcross stock that had already proved its worth. Most of the colts that are marked for possible use in the breeding program are ridden by the Kineños, and they must gain the wholehearted approval of the riders before they are put into the brood-mare bands. On the King Ranch all horses are owned by the ranch, and no Kineño can ride his own horse while he is working. The horses of the remudas are distributed to the Kineños by the *caporal,* or local foreman. When a horse makes good and is returned to the breeding program, the particular Kineño who rode the mare has first call on her offspring. This prerogative is much appreciated by the men, and a lot of good-natured rivalry exists among the men and their mounts. Horse breeding on the King Ranch is a small part of the over-all picture, but few people would call breeding, training, and using some two thousand Quarter Horses an insignificant endeavor. On the ranch there are many people who spend most of their time with the Quarter Horses.

In general, the breeding plan for the ranch Quarter Horses followed a concurrent program being conducted with the cattle, a program which resulted in the development of the Santa Gertrudis breed. Bob Kleberg fixed the desired characteristics for the Santa Gertrudis, in the mold of the great sire Monkey. He used five-eighths Brahma and three-eighths Shorthorn to combine the best features of both. Monkey was branded in 1920 and was turned in with his first breeding heifers in 1923. The Old Sorrel was purchased in 1916, and the horse-breeding program was begun in 1921. If the American Quarter Horse Association had not been established in 1940, the King Ranch would undoubtedly have become known as the only ranch in history to create two new breeds of livestock, the Santa Gertrudis and the King Ranch Sorrel Horses.

To complete the story of the King Ranch breeding program, the following pages are devoted to an account of the program by the person now responsible for making the decisions, Richard M. Kleberg, Jr.:

I was born on the Laureles Division of King Ranch and lived there until I was eight years old. My father was then in charge of this division. He showed keen interest not only in the cattle but also in the horse stock. He was very fond of the Sunday afternoon "cotton row" races and won quite a few with Laureles raised horses.

We moved to Corpus Christi, where we children could attend grade school, but every summer until I went to college was spent on the Ranch.

Following my graduation from college in 1940, I have worked for and with R. J. Kleberg, Jr., and the King Ranch.

Under the guidance of my father and uncle, I acquired quite a bit of practical knowledge concerning the qualities looked for in the working horse.

I also learned during those years, by observation, that the men that work with and train their own mounts do not "break" a horse but that the good horseman "makes" a horse.

Some horses tend to be "natural" stock horses, just as some men are natural athletes. This trait has proven to be heritable to a certain degree, particularly if you (as an individual) look for this trait and select for it.

This practice was started by my two aforementioned relatives in selecting the stallions and the mares to be used in the Ranch breeding program.

I guess you might say that, through my keen interest in the Quarter Horses, I acquired most of my ability to select individuals to enter the breeding program through osmosis.

Over the years since 1940, Bob Kleberg became and is quite busy with the foreign developments and expansions of King Ranch Texas, and more and more of the selection of Quarter Horses to enter the breeding program was left to me. However, I must add that whenever he (Bob) disagreed with my selection, I stood corrected. I must add, happily, that these disagreements have been very few.

Naturally, it has become much easier to select on the basis of conformation because of the close attention paid to this important detail by Bob Kleberg's earlier selections.

In every breed society there is a definite distinction between the so-

146

called "fine" points and the breed character and performance of the individual.

What I try to look for in an individual that has the potential to enter the breeding program is first conformation—head, neck, withers, legs, muscles, temperament and size.

We keep all individuals that pass this first test until they are old enough to observe them under saddle. Naturally, if we have four good sons of an outstanding sire, we attempt to select the best two, hoping that one of these will prove himself in performance—the best will enter the breeding program—the other will be gelded.

If we have only one good son by an aged stallion (in his last crop of colts), we will retain him, hoping he proves himself in performance.

Mares selected for the breeding program are chosen in preference to others in many ways. First there has to be the ability of performance. The performance is sometimes not considered in a young mare that was in the process of being trained but received some injury and is considered not sound of wind or legs or any of the various injuries that can and do occur in training. Then only her parentage is considered, providing, of course, her conformation is good and her dam a good individual. These fillies are then considered as prospective breeding stock. However, if their progeny do not measure up, they are removed and disposed of or if gentle enough and sound enough for light riding, are turned over to the family or the cowboys' children to ride.

For the proven mares the story is somewhat different. The performance, conformation, and bloodlines all come into effect. For instance take a hypothetical case. You have, body-wise, a perfect conformation mare, but her head is a little coarse. Then, if bloodlines do not interfere, you breed her to the best-headed horse in hopes that the progeny of this mare are improved by the horse. With bloodline to consider, each proven mare is bred to a horse that has the best points of the least desirable points in the mare.

If these unions do not produce at least an individual as good as the dam, she is bred to a different animal. Then and only then, if she continues to produce inferior progeny to our standards by King Ranch stallions, she is removed from the breeding program. If she is young and sound enough, she is returned to the *remuda*, or made into a kid pony.

147

On King Ranch we now have nine separate breeding-mare bands. Seven of these stallions go back directly to Hired Hand on the sire side. Of the other two, one goes back to Rey del Rancho and the other to Wimpy.

As an example of what I've tried to say, I have picked eleven mares at random which are now being bred to Mendigo. His pedigree is given [below].

Seven of the above-mentioned are by Rey del Rancho. They were selected not only on conformation and performance but on bloodlines because many of our Ranch mares trace back even within the third generation to Hired Hand.[5] Breeding Mendigo to these particular mares gives us what you could call an outcross within the King Ranch family of Quarter Horses.

Anita Chica—by Rey del Rancho. She is out of an outstanding roping and cutting mare. She likewise is a top cutting mare and very heavily muscled.

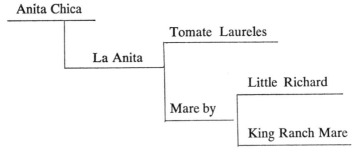

Fantasma—by Rey del Rancho. She is also very heavily muscled and a top cutting mare. This mare has had eleven foals by different sires all going back to Hired Hand.

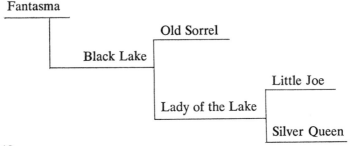

148

Faustina Rey—by Rey del Rancho. She is a top cutting mare.

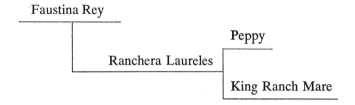

Pagadora—by Rey del Rancho. She is a very good roping mare.

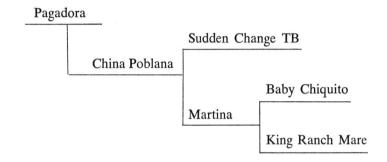

Pera de Andres—by Rey del Rancho. She is a good roping mare.

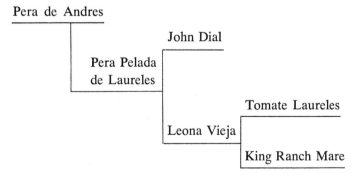

[5] Dick Kleberg wrote the author as follows: "You will note that Mendigo's pedigree and those of most of the mares on the dam side go back to dams and sires that are not of King Ranch breeding. I made the comment about an outcross within the King Ranch family of horses because of this." Letter dated March 21, 1968, Denhardt Files, R. M. Kleberg, Jr., Folder.

La Perrita—by Rey del Rancho. She is very heavy-set and a good roping mare.

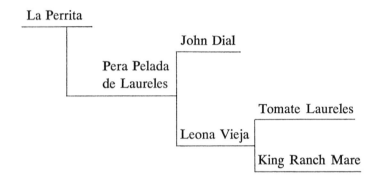

Playhouse Ninety—by Rey del Rancho. She is a very good cutting mare.

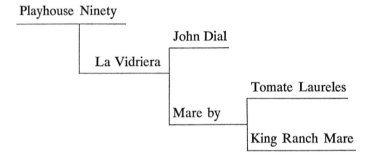

Flor Sylvestre—by Hired Hand's Cardinal. She is a good cutting and roping mare.

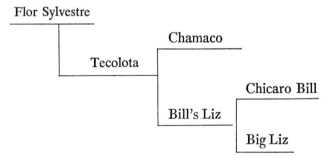

150

Pal Chiquita—by Hired Hand. She is a very good and fast roping mare.

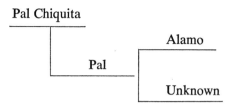

Sandia de Chale—by Peppy. She is a very heavy-set good roping mare.

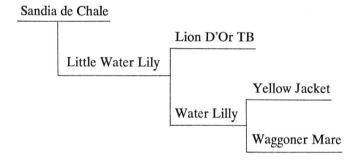

La Tuna—by Hired Hand. She is a good roping mare.

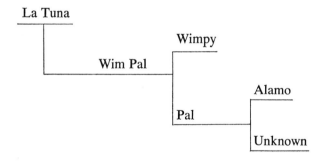

151

QUARTER HORSE PEDIGREE

Name: MENDIGO   Reg.No. P-143,772

Color: Red Chestnut   Sex: Stallion   Year Foaled: 1960

Breeder: King Ranch   Address: Kingsville, Texas

Owner: King Ranch   Address: Kingsville, Texas

CARDENAL CHICO P-63,951 — Sire

- HIRED HAND'S CARDINAL P-38,194
  - HIRED HAND P-2495
    - OLD SORREL P-209
    - WATER LILLY P-168
  - LISTONA AZULE P-6460
    - PEPPY P-212
    - LISTONA P-197
- LA BROOKS P-27,085
  - MACANUDO P-211
    - OLD SORREL P-209
    - CANALES BELL P-141
  - BARCA DE ORA P-6416
    - TINO P-214
    - #7 ROAN CLEGG MARE

Markings: Large irr. star, elongated faint snip

HIJA DE MENDIGA P-61,431 — Dam

- HIRED HAND P-2495
  - OLD SORREL P-209
    - HICKORY BILL
    - DR. ROSE MARE
  - WATER LILLY P-168
    - YELLOW JACKET
    - WAGGONER MARE
- MENDIGA P-6467
  - ONE TENTH TB
    - *COHORT TB
    - SUNSET GUN TB
  - MEDALLA P-160
    - RANCHERO P-215
    - HERMANA CACHOS

This horse shows more of the TB type, as you can see he should because of his pedigree.

Early each fall (September if possible) I go through all of the brood mares and inspect and brand the foals—they are classified into three general categories—Top, Good, Fair; these are based on conformation. I try to look at all of them within three or four days' time in order to keep my "eye in," so to speak. I make comments concerning good and bad traits or faults.

The tops are retained for the Ranch until they prove or disprove themselves under the saddle. From the good group are selected the sale animals (auction or private treaty). The fair group (colts castrated) are used for cow horses, and possibly some *few* of the geldings are sold.

After this classification I go back over my notes as soon as possible and determine if some mare should be bred to a different stallion next season, particularly if she is a good individual but did not produce a better than fair foal.[6]

6 Statement attached to letter dated March 21, 1968, Denhardt Files, R. M. Kleberg, Jr., Folder.

PART III

24. Wimpy P-1

Part I of this book was concerned with the beginnings of the King Ranch, its people, and its horses. Part II examined the origin of the King Ranch Quarter Horses and their breeding. Part III will deal with some of the individual horses that have gained fame and with some of the men who have showed and raced King Ranch horses.

Since colonial days racing Quarter Horses have furnished the cowman with his best stallions because of their quiet dispositions and early speed. When the short-horse stallions were crossed on the native cow-horse mares (predominantly of Spanish and Mexican origin), the resulting offspring had everything the cowman wanted: cow sense, disposition, and early speed.

In the late 1930's and early 1940's short racing was still popular in the ranch country of the Southwest, as it had been since the times of the early settlers. With the organization of the American Quarter Horse Association and its absorption of the American Quarter Racing Association in 1949, the number of short races on rural straightways dwindled. In several states the development of pari-mutuel betting on Quarter Horse races eliminated the demand for rural tracks. For many years the King Ranch maintained a race track and rodeo ground at the edge of Kingsville. Today it has been converted into a real-estate addition. The ranch still maintains its own track and barns on the Santa Gertrudis. But in earlier days the old ranch track at Kingsville and others like it were hosts to most of the famous South Texas short-horses at one time or another. Horses like Little Joe, Zantanon, and King ran match races and then entered the stud. Some of these speed merchants became very popular and sired outstanding sons and daughters, many of whom found their way into the King Ranch cow-horse remudas by way of the outcross mares. So Quarter racing and Quarter Horse breeding have been intertwined throughout the years. Sprinting Thoroughbred blood has been used by some Quarter Horse breeders. Bob Kleberg was especially successful in combining the right amount and the right type of Thoroughbred blood. The King Ranch horses have maintained their cow sense and their quiet disposition.

IN THE EARLY SPRING of 1935, a stocky little sorrel colt was foaled on the King Ranch and was named Wimpy. Little did those who first saw him realize that this colt was soon to typify the American Quarter Horse to the American public and that he was to have the honor of being registered number 1 in the *Stud Book and Registry* of the American Quarter Horse Association.

When the officials of the association began registering Quarter Horses, they started at 20. Number 20, the first horse actually registered, belonged to Bill Warren and his brother, John. Bill Warren was the first president of the American Quarter Horse Association. The stallion registered was Pancho, who was by Paul El, a half brother of the Old Sorrel. Pancho was out of a Little Joe mare. The first nineteen places were reserved for foundation animals. The reader should not be surprised to learn that the King Ranch is the only breeder, and the Old Sorrel the only stallion, with more than one representation in this exclusive group. Tomate Laureles is registered number 19, Little Richard registered number 17, and Wimpy, number 1.

Wimpy had earned his right to the number 1 spot even before he had a chance to prove his great worth as a sire. There were famous horses living in 1940–41. Joe Bailey, Joe Hancock, Zantanon, Joe Reed, and even Oklahoma Star were all much older and better known. Wimpy won his right to the number by being judged the outstanding horse at the Southwestern Exposition and Fat Stock Show held in Fort Worth in 1941. At the time the newly formed Quarter Horse Association was struggling to get off the ground. One idea that seemed to promise additional inducement to breeders to register and show their horses was to give the number 1 spot in the *Stud Book* to the grand-champion stallion. The idea caught fire, and outstanding horses from all over the West came to the Fort Worth show. Most of the horses were from Texas, of course, but Marshall Peavy, of Clark, Colorado, and Jack Casement, of Whitewater, Colorado, entered horses in the show, as did Elmer Hepler, of New Mexico. A large group came from Oklahoma. Most western states were represented. There was a remarkable group of stallions from which the judge, James H. Minnick, of Crowell, Texas, had to select a champion. Jim Minnick, one of the few really great all-around horsemen of his day, was the official judge for the fledgling horse association. He judged all the early official shows, and more than anyone else he was responsible for setting the type of horse the association was looking for. He could hardly have done better than name Wimpy the winner, as subsequent years have proved.

The first horse to enter the show ring that day was Silvertone, led by his proud owner, Lee Underwood, of Wichita Falls. Silvertone was a beautiful golden palomino and a born crowd pleaser. Next came one of the most promising young stallions in the nation, Little Joe Jr. He was by Gonzales Joe Bailey and had been the grand-champion cow-horse stallion at the Tucson show in 1942. He had also established an enviable racing record. Little Joe Jr. followed his owner, Larry Baumer, of Utopia, Texas, as a good Quarter Horse should—quietly. But his little fox ears were working. Another horse that caused a ripple of excitement was a sleek, athletic dun, running sideways on his halter. He was Silver Dawn, bred by the Waggoner Ranch. Silver Dawn was sired by Clover Leaf and out of a Rainy Day mare. He was being shown by J. V. Frye, a topnotch Quarter Horse breeder from Woodward, Oklahoma.

Wimpy came in soon after Silver Dawn. He seemed to float as he came into the arena. He was bouncing on his pasterns like a deer on the alert, moving in a sort of stylized trot. He carried his head low, and his eyes and ears were taking in everything. He was led by Lauro Cavazos, who seemed to ignore Wimpy as he walked around the arena.

Each stallion came out in turn and joined the circling parade. Jim

Minnick watched them for a while, moved them individually, and then lined them up and studied each horse. After rearranging them several times, he finally left the arena. He had placed them as follows: Wimpy, Silvertone, Red Jacket, Little Joe Jr., Top Flight, and Silver Dawn. So it was that Wimpy won his number 1 spot in the *Stud Book*.

Since he was sired by Solis and not the Old Sorrel, Wimpy belongs to the group of second-generation stallions. Wimpy's dam, Panda, was a daughter of the Old Sorrel. Her dam was a mare sired by Hickory Bill, making her a half sister of the Old Sorrel. The Old Sorrel was thus bred to his half sister, and the result was Panda. Then Panda was bred to her half brother, Solis, and the result was Wimpy. In his bloodlines Wimpy was therefore one-half Old Sorrel, one-fourth Lazarus Thoroughbred, and, the other fourth, one-half Quarter Horse and one-half Hickory Bill.

Breeding half sisters to half brothers may seem a little tight—and it does make Wimpy inbred. Inbreeding can be a dangerous procedure for the average breeder working with only thirty or forty mares and three or four stallions. It appears, however, that, when it is practiced by a master breeder and geneticist such as Bob Kleberg, it works. Careful culling and intelligent and intuitive selection of individuals encourages success, and the desired characteristics are thereby doubled and tripled until they are set.

Wimpy proved to be a great breeder, and he produced many great sons and daughters. The best were retained by the King Ranch, and their excellence and their reputation is known only locally. Some of his offspring were sold to members of the general public, however, and they gained justifiable fame. They have been entered in various shows and performance classes and have attracted notice, winning more than their share of events. In all Wimpy sired about two hundred sons and daughters that were registered by the American Quarter Horse Association. Today the descendants of these registered offspring are legion. For example, there is, or was, Bill Cody, owned by Glen Casey; Little Wimpy, owned by Roy Parks; Candy, Jr., owned by Loyd Jinkens; Wimpy II, owned by John Dawson; Silver Wimpy, owned by Clarence Scarbauer; Cabra's Wimpy, owned by William Thompson; Showdown, owned by O. G. Hill, Jr.; and Red Wimpy, owned by A. C. Perks.

A list of the show- and performance-contest winners would run into

160

the hundreds. Some idea of Wimpy's success as a sire can be gained by reviewing the history of one stallion he sired, AQHA Champion Bill Cody. In turn Bill Cody sired eight AQHA champions. Two of Bill Cody's sons, Lauro and Wimpy II, each sired five AQHA champions. In addition, two of Wimpy's sons and two of his grandsons were listed by AQHA among the leading sires of point-earning performance horses.[1] Bill Cody is listed among the leading sires of "show register of merit" qualifiers. Altogether, the King Ranch had a total of 103 qualifiers and 40 AQHA champions, mostly through Wimpy. This number accounts for about one-eighth of the total produced by the best 30 Quarter Horses in the nation (incidentally, the ranch contributed almost one-fourth of all the AQHA champions in the list of outstanding horses).

To conclude Wimpy's story, a quotation from Garford Wilkinson is in order. When Wimpy was twenty-three years old, he was given to George Clegg. Wilkinson said, "No greater tribute could have been paid by the Kleberg family to a noble friend than their gift in 1958 of Wimpy P-1 to George Clegg, who had bred this great stallion's grandsire."[2] Because of illness Clegg was later forced to part with Wimpy, who was sold to Rex Cauble, of Houston. As Wilkinson said, Wimpy spent his last days knee-deep in clover, with all the love and care man could provide. He died on August 14, 1959.

1 *Quarter Horse Journal*, May, 1967, 16–28.
2 "Dedication of a Statue," *Quarter Horse Journal*, November, 1961, 28.

25. Peppy P-212

Peppy P-212, an outstanding sorrel stallion, was born on the ranch in the spring of 1934, six years before the American Quarter Horse Association was established. Peppy's popularity in horse shows did much to help engender interest in the Quarter Horse and gave added impetus to the drive for a Quarter Horse studbook.

Peppy was a son of Little Richard and out of a daughter of Cardenal. Both Little Richard and Cardenal, out of Thoroughbred mares, had been sired by the Old Sorrel. When Peppy matured, he stood 15 hands ½ inch high and in good flesh weighed 1,204 pounds. He died in Wyoming on February 24, 1964.

The Gregg Ranch, at Big Horn, Wyoming, where Peppy died, is a long way from the Santa Gertrudis. He lived a full and fruitful life, however, and if he traveled far, his reputation traveled farther. His influence on the Quarter Horse has been considerable, and it continues to grow each year as his sons and grandsons, daughters and granddaughters produce outstanding progeny. On his grave lies a simple stone, which gives merely his name and the dates of his birth and death. Anything more would be superfluous. The marker can be found under a tree where Peppy used to stand and doze and switch his tail at the flies. No doubt he dreamed as he dozed, probably about the cactus- and mesquite-covered brush country of South Texas where he grew to maturity.

162

Miss Princess

Miss Princess, with Dr. J. K. Northway at the halter. Foaled in 1943, she was sired
by Bold Venture and out of Bruja by Livery. Miss Princess was a registered Thoroughbred under the name of Woven Web. She showed real speed racing in
Mexico, and Robert J. Kleberg, Jr., gave her to Ernest Lane to run. She became
World's Champion Running Quarter Horse until she was retired in 1948.

John Dial

John Dial, foaled in 1937, was one of Ada Jones's great sons. This bay colt by Chicaro was named for John W. Dial, of Goliad, from whom Robert J. Kleberg, Jr., had bought both her sire and her dam. Eight of John Dial's fillies were placed in the Quarter Horse breeding program.

Lady Speck and Don Manners

The match race held between Lady Speck (foreground) and Don Manners in Kingsville in 1939 (Chapter 17). The race illustrated the friendly rivalry between the grandsons of Richard King and Mifflin Kenedy. Robert J. Kleberg, Jr., owned Don Manners, and John Kenedy owned Lady Speck. Lady Speck barely beat Don Manners at the finish.

Don Manners

Don Manners working out of the gates at Eagle Pass. He was foaled in 1936 and was sired by the Remount Service stallion Lovely Manners and out of Chicaro Jane. Although a registered Thoroughbred, he ran well as a Quarter Horse at Eagle Pass and at Tucson.

Don Manners having his legs wrapped. This picture was taken in Tucson in 1943.

Chicaro

Chicaro, foaled in 1923, was imported *Chicle and out of Wendy by Peter Pan. He has had more influence on the King Ranch breeding program than any other stallion except the Old Sorrel. The ranch used twenty mares by Chicaro in its program. This picture was taken in 1936.

Nobody's Friend

Nobody's Friend was the Champion Racing Quarter Horse Stallion at Tucson in 1942. Foaled in 1939, he was the product of crossing Boojum, one of the fastest Thoroughbreds of all time, with the Quarter mare Pal. He had an erratic temperament, but only Shue Fly could beat him, in record time, for the World's Championship in 1942. Here he is being led around before his famous match race with Clabber in Eagle Pass in 1941 (Chapter 15).

Depth Charge

Depth Charge, foaled in 1941, was a brown Thoroughbred stallion sired by Bold Venture. His dam was Quickly by Haste. He was a half brother of Miss Princess (Woven Web). Five of his fillies found their way into the Quarter Horse program.

Remolino

Remolino, foaled in 1934, was a bay Thoroughbred stallion sired by Ariel, a stallion noted for his early speed and Quarter-type conformation. Remolino's dam was Flying Dust by High Cloud. During World War II many soldiers from nearby airfields and army camps visited the ranch to see the horses.

Lovely Manners

Lovely Manners, foaled in 1924, was a Thoroughbred Remount stallion kept for a time by Richard Kleberg. He was by Sweep by Ben Brush and out of Lady Sournoise. Five mares by Lovely Manners were used in the ranch breeding program.

Peppy was one year older than Wimpy. Wimpy may have been well known to serious Quarter Horse breeders, but to the general public Peppy was Mr. Quarter Horse. Peppy was also generally considered the better individual of the two by most experts who observed both horses in their early days on the ranch. Hazel Oatman Bowman, writing in 1940, described Peppy as the "top stallion of the King Ranch special breed of cow horses. He is an outstanding individual; has worked the quarter mile in 22.2 seconds. Peppy was grand champion Quarter Horse Stallion at the 1940 Southwestern Exposition and Fat Stock Show."[1]

The following year, 1941, Wimpy was sent to Fort Worth to represent the ranch and was named grand champion. Many experts believed that Peppy was a better show animal than Wimpy because he had a little more quality and refinement. If that is true, then if Peppy had been sent to the show in 1941 he would have been number 1 in the *Stud Book and Registry*. George Clegg, who showed many of the King Ranch horses about the time the AQHA was organized, always said that he favored Peppy.

Peppy was such an outstanding individual that Bob Kleberg decided he would be a good horse to exhibit as an example of the type and kind of cow horse the ranch was raising. Thus Peppy became the first of the King Ranch strain to be shown extensively. He made an auspicious start at the Texas Centennial in Dallas in 1936. Dr. Northway loaded some Santa Gertrudis cattle, two or three mares, and Peppy and took them north to the centennial. When they were unloaded and led across the grounds to their stalls, the excitement they caused was merely a preliminary to the sensation they made among the thousands of persons who saw for the first time the cherry-red Santa Gertrudis cattle and the beautiful red sorrel horses of the King Ranch.

For the next five years Peppy was frequently exhibited and entered in show classes in the larger expositions and livestock shows across the country. He won literally a barrelful of ribbons and roomsful of statues and medals. Seemingly he could not lose a class, and he was almost invariably the grand champion and best individual in the show. Peppy finished his show career at the 1941 Tucson Horse Show, held in connection with the Tucson Live-

[1] Hazel Oatman Bowman, "King Ranch Horse," *Cattleman*, September, 1940, 82.

163

stock Show. There he was named grand-champion cow horse before such a show was held for Quarter Horses. He was the first Texas horse to win the title. After the Tucson show Bob Kleberg decided to take Peppy home and put him to work for the ranch.

To no one's surprise, Peppy also proved to be outstanding in the stud. He has about two hundred registered get in the books of the Quarter Horse Association. Though Peppy is especially noted for the mares he sired, he produced some outstanding stallions as well, for example, the brilliant Peppy's Pepper, whose dam, Cubana, foaled him in 1944. He was sold as a yearling to Loyd Jinkens, of Fort Worth. In 1946, Jinkens sold him for $26,500, the highest price paid for a Quarter Horse to that time. Garford Wilkinson, writing in 1966, said that "horsemen say that Peppy's Pepper, many times champion in an era prior to the preservation of show records, was singularly superior and virtually unbeatable as a three-year-old."[2]

August Busch, of St. Louis, did his best to buy Peppy while the horse was in his prime. Dr. Northway commented about the effort, saying that Busch asked Bob Kleberg for a refusal price. "But Mr. Kleberg declined to part with Peppy, who was at that time an integral part of the ranch's breeding program. He did, however, offer to sell a son of Peppy to Mr. Busch at a nominal price."[3]

As Peppy grew up on the ranch, he was handled exactly like every other colt. He was broken, ridden, and trained as a cow horse. At the ranch round-ups he showed a natural talent for cutting and roping. During much of this time Dick Kleberg rode him. Most fillies by Peppy had his talent for cow work, and were therefore put back into the brood-mare bands. Peppy's horse colts were in particular demand and found their way into the breeding herds of many important institutions, such as Washington State University, Chicago University, and Michigan State University. Many prominent individuals also bought his colts. Peppy's American Girl was bought by the University of Illinois. She was later repurchased by the ranch, which had to pay $2,350 to get her back.

In 1946, when Peppy was twelve years old, he was loaned to a friend

2 Garford Wilkinson, "Peppy P–212," *Quarter Horse Journal,* October, 1966, 29.
3 *Ibid.,* 29.

of the Klebergs, Alex Gregg, of Birney, Montana (later of Sheridan, Wyoming). Gregg used Peppy for one season and then returned him to the ranch, as agreed. Gregg was overjoyed to get a 100 per cent colt crop. Seven years later he asked Bob Kleberg if he could borrow Peppy again. By that time Peppy was nineteen years old, and the ranch had sufficient sons and daughters by him. They agreed to lend Peppy to Gregg once more.

For years Peppy had been pasture-bred to a manada of forty mares but he was now getting too old for this method. Gregg kept him up and bred him by hand. When Gregg died, his widow disposed of the ranch and moved the horses to a smaller spread near Big Horn, Wyoming. In speaking about Peppy's life at Big Horn, she said, "I think he was happier here than at the Sheridan Ranch. He had a nice paddock with plenty of green grass, trees, and a blanket when needed, a nice warm stall at night with a young filly in the stall next to him."[4]

One well-known Peppy mare was Cacuchia. Bob Kleberg gave her to J. Frank Norfleet, of Hale Center, Texas, in return for a favor Norfleet had once done for the ranch when he was a Texas Ranger. Cacuchia had been bred to Wimpy and had foaled a stud colt, named Showdown. He was purchased by O. G. Hill, Jr. Showdown was a great individual and was successful in both performance and halter classes. When he was retired from the show ring, he became an outstanding sire. He has well over three hundred registered get, and he ranks as one of the greatest of the Quarter Horse breed. In 1965 he was fourth among the leading Sires of Halter Class Winners and sixth among the leaders for the Get of Sire winners. When one realizes how few animals there are of this class among the thousands of registered animals, his performance becomes impressive.

Another son of Peppy, Peppy's Pokey, foaled in 1946, became widely known in the Middle West. He was sold to Ed Chudik, of Bloomfield, Illinois. Chudik showed Peppy's Pokey at many of the best shows in the country, and he easily won a Register of Merit ranking and also received an AQHA Championship award. Many other sons and grandsons of Peppy also received both titles, among them Strawboss T, Illini King Hand, and Henry's Bullet.

[4] *Ibid.*, 56.

Peppy sired Listona Azule, the dam of Hired Hand's Cardinal. He also sired La Perdita, the dam of Hired Hand II. Both Hired Hand II and Hired Hand's Cardinal have played an important part in the ranch's Quarter Horse program.

Peppy's place in the annals of the Quarter Horse breed is secure.

26. Short-Horses and Ernest Lane

ERNEST LANE was closely connected with one important facet of the King Ranch cow-horse program: the maintenance of early speed in the horses. One of the most desirable characteristics of a good cow horse is his ability to catch or turn an animal before he runs half a mile or disappears into the brush. The Klebergs loved a horse race and delighted in raising faster horses than those their friends and neighbors were producing. The story of Miss Princess (Chapter 27) is an excellent illustration. Bob Kleberg had other reasons for participating in horse races, however. For one thing, he wanted to be sure that the Thoroughbred blood he was putting into his Quarter Horses was adding to their early speed. Miss Princess, Nobody's Friend, and others convinced him that he was using the right Thoroughbred bloodlines in his program. Nobody's Friend was named World's Champion Racing Stallion in 1942, and Miss Princess became World's Champion Quarter Running Horse in 1947. Other Thoroughbreds and half Thoroughbreds used to check bloodlines were Mickie (Witchbrew), Maggie (Chovasco), and Don Manners.

Since Bob Kleberg could not leave the ranch to train and run short-horses himself, he searched for someone who could do the job for him. At first he sent some horses with George Clegg, but neither George nor Bob was happy with the arrangement. Kleberg knew Ernest Lane, who was very

167

successful as a short-horse man, and he decided that Lane was the man he needed to train and run King Ranch horses.

Ernest Lane lived a few miles north of the ranch at Odem, Texas. He had been familiar with the ranch ever since he was a young man, when he had cut firewood on the Santa Gertrudis. The Lane family moved to South Texas when the owners of the Taft Ranch near Odem broke up their ranch and sold it in parcels for cotton farming. In 1911 Lane's father was one of the first to buy some of the land. As the years went by, Lane acquired some cotton land of his own and gradually increased his holdings until he owned both farm land and ranch property.

The following account of Ernest Lane and his activities in connection with the King Ranch is given substantially in Lane's own words, except for the deletion of material not pertinent to this book and of certain colorful expressions. Here and there words and phrases have been added for the benefit of the reader unacquainted with South Texas short-horse terminology. But the flavor of Ernest Lane's speech comes through:

> I never really started to race short-horses; they just sort of built up. I got one horse, and then I got another. I knew Ott Adams. I went over to see him one day, and he had a beautiful colt out of a good King Ranch mare. This was Bumps and his mother. I wanted that colt, but Ott said, "That colt is spoken for." I asked Ott how much he was getting for the colt, and he said, "Three fifty." After a while I said, "I'll give you five hundred dollars for it right now," and that did the job.
>
> I had a pretty good size ranch down by Odem, and I just took him down there and let him run for a while. I kept him down there till he was a two-year-old—had a boy handling him, and he was gentle when I brought him into town. I let this boy go on handling him in town, and he got to running him. A wild bunch of kids had horses, and he was running them with Bumps. These kids ran him down the turn rows— some might be a quarter of a mile long, some might be a mile long.
>
> It's sort of interesting how he got his name. When I got ready to take him home, I roped him, and he came right over backwards, and he fell on his tail, and it broke it, and he had a little bump right at the head of the tail, and that's where he got his name. One day the boy, Gillespie, came up and said, "You know, Mr. Lane, this little horse Bumps can

168

really run. None of the boys can even run close to me." I said "Boy, you're going to spoil that horse running him so much." He said, "Oh, I'm not running him much." I found out afterwards he was running him every time the boys got together.

Then I bought some mares from Elijío García down in the valley. Among them were Flicka and Sugar Baby. Flicka holds a track record at Eagle Pass in 15 flat. She could not run that fast, of course. They must have looked at their watch and had it wrong because they aren't running that fast now. It was probably sixteen. Anyway, that's how I got started.

They had that old race track down in Kingsville. I used to race down there, and I raced Bob Kleberg. Everybody showed up at Kingsville—Alonzo Taylor, Banks Barbee, and the Louisiana bunch. Bob Kleberg wanted to match that old black horse he called Nobody's Friend. And he had Johnny Armstrong, one of the best short-horse trainers there was in Texas. Johnny had Lady of the Lake.

I told Bob I couldn't run a quarter of a mile against Nobody's Friend or anybody else. Bob wanted to know how far I would run, and I said 250 yards. He said, "All right."

Alonzo Taylor had a one-eyed horse that he called I'll Go, and I also had a mare called Flo. I had bought her in Louisiana to run against Shue Fly. Ab Simpson took me over to Louisiana. While I was looking at this mare, they put one of those Cajun boys on her. I guess he weighed probably forty pounds dripping wet. They backed her into place, and then they just hollered, "Go!" I clocked that damn mare in 15.5. I always clock my horses slow. This way I would have an advantage when I matched. In my own horses I always tried to catch on the saddle of the horse, not on the nose. After Flo had run this 15.5, I told Ab Simpson, "That mare ran pretty fast. I caught her in 16 flat."

Ab said, "Well you didn't catch her right. I caught her in 15.8."

I said, "Why don't you try to buy her for me?" They wanted $750, but I hauled her away for $600. I brought Flo back and let her rest for about two weeks and then began training her. When she was really ready to run, I decided to run her against Bumps. Now Bumps could run 300 and maybe 350, but he'd be beat if he ran any further. At 250 just nobody could beat him. She almost did. Soon after that I matched five

169

races with Theobart Comiere. Comiere asked what horses I was going to run. I said, "I'm not asking you what horses you're going to run. You just gather together the five best horses from Louisiana and bring them down here to Skidmore, and I'll have five Texas horses, and we'll run."

We agreed on the distances. I was going to run my horses the way I wanted to, and he was to run his the way he wanted to. I ran Bumps, Flicka, Skippy, Maggie, and Sugar Baby. Everybody over there went by what Theobart said. He's the one, you know, who sold Jack Hutchins his good horses. It was all catch weights. I tied one, lost one, and won the rest of them. I lost one race out of five. Joy Weakly, of Wharton, was one of the judges on the race I lost. I think he made an honest mistake. He said Mae West won that race. When he did, his wife just about beat him down. She said that Flicka won the race. Most of the people there thought Flicka did win, including Charles Stegall and his wife and Roy Gaines and his wife.

Old Joy Weakly was really a character. We used to call him "spit in the track." He used to keep some fast horses. He and Dink Bishop, of Wharton, used to love to match races. We would say, "How far do you want to run?" when he had a horse to match, and he'd say, "You just spit in the track."

But let's get back to Kleberg and the King Ranch. I told Bob that I had a mare here named Flo from Louisiana. "If Alonzo Taylor will give me a race, we'll just have two races here next Sunday." He said that Alonzo would run me. So we matched Flo against I'll Go for a quarter of a mile, and Bumps against Nobody's Friend for 250. I won both races. Then Bob Kleberg said, "Ernest, we'll just run you again next week, but next week I'm going to run you a quarter of a mile."

I told Bob, "I just can't run Bumps a quarter of a mile. He never was a quarter-of-a-mile horse. Three-fifty's as far as I liked to go with him. I wouldn't even go that far if I hadn't won a race off you." However, Bob wanted to run me a quarter. Finally I said, "All right, then, but just for the same money—I'm not going to do any betting on the side with you."

So we matched it for $500, just like we'd matched the other. We had bet a $1,000 on the side on the race that I had won, but I wasn't going to bet anything on the side on this race. And actually, Bob wasn't

170

much for betting. He never did bet very much on his horses. There was a big crowd there. The Mexicans built up a high place for his horse to start on. They thought that he would come running downhill faster, but a horse starts with his head up, and it is hard for a horse to get his head up when he is coming downhill. When his back end's up too high, he's really got problems.

Graves Peeler was starting them, and he said that the horses weren't going to start good off this hill. Bob didn't care how they started. He just wanted to see which was the fastest. I told Graves, "Just open the gates whenever you catch Bumps with his two hind feet together and looking forward."

Pretty quick he opened the gate. Before anyone knew it, Bumps was daylight ahead of the black horse. Bob had told the Mexican to go to the bat if he got behind. So when Bumps got ahead, the Mexican reached back and gave his horse a good cut with the quirt, and when he did, Nobody's Friend bucked that Mexican off as high as a ceiling.

When I talked to Bob, I said, "I'm not going to take your money. It wasn't a good race." However, Bob said, "Yes, you are going to take the money. I lost that race." Then he said, "When you can bring your short-horses out here and beat my horses, there must be something to your training. I'm glad I at least bred the dam of your horse Bumps."

I used to keep going down to Kingsville a lot, and sometime later —I don't know when it was—six months, maybe—he told me to come on down, and we would select some horses, and I could race them in my own name, and when I got through with them, I was to bring them back. They were mine while I was racing them.

Bob Kleberg is the best man I ever knew. He's just the best I ever had anything to do with. You'd be surprised if I told you what he's done for me. He gave me Top Deck, for example. I sold him for $25,000.

Miss Princess was a beautiful two-year-old. She'd been down in Mexico running for Bob. She set a record down in Mexico of 21⅘ or something for a quarter mile. She bowed a tendon, and they sent her back to the ranch. They brought her back and worked on her, and I was down there one day when Bob said, "We're going to work a mare. Let's time her." Bob said that he thought this was the mare that was going to outrun Shue Fly.

I said, "Well, Bob, maybe, but it's going to take a hell of a mare." Bob replied, "This is a hell of a mare."

So we went down to the track. They put an exercise saddle on her that weighed about three pounds and then about a thirty-five-pound Mexican—not much over forty-five pounds at the most. Bob suggested that we go down to the quarter pole and time her. I told him to go down to the quarter pole because I was going to catch her here, halfway.

Well, she ran the eighth awful fast, I'll tell you. Then Bob said, "Ernest, she's your mare, now let's run Shue Fly." That's how it all started.[1]

1 Denhardt Files, King Ranch Tapes, reel No. 2.

27. Miss Princess

A QUARTER of a century ago two foals were born on the King Ranch, both sired by Bold Venture. One was destined to win more money than any horse that had lived and run before him, despite trouble with a foot (caused by pawing at a surveyor's stake) that would have eliminated a horse of lesser heart. The other, an affectionate little sorrel filly, made her name on the short tracks as the champion who beat the seemingly indomitable Shue Fly. The sorrel filly needed no further glory after that win to become a legend, but she did not stop there. To remove all doubt that her great race was not a fluke, she began a systematic assault upon existing Quarter Horse records. They fell before her like clay pigeons at a trap shoot. She was aptly named Miss Princess.

Miss Princess began life like any other foal on the King Ranch, frolicking and playing with the other colts in the pasture. She was registered in the Jockey Club as Woven Web. Her dam was Bruja by Livery out of Chicaro's Hallie by Chicaro. Chicaro's Hallie, her granddam, had had a most interesting record. The first time she raced, she was lined up beside a horse that had broken the track record at Tanforan, and her price was eighty-two dollars for a two-dollar ticket. Chicaro's Hallie won the race by three lengths of daylight. When Miss Princess's dam Bruja came along, she too won her first start, and one of her opponents was the great Ciencia, who won the

Santa Anita Derby. Miss Princess followed in their footsteps, winning her first four starts in Mexico.

Bob Kleberg expected great things from Miss Princess, and she did her best. Her first big-time performance in Mexico City was the talk of the town. In five starts she won four races and placed in the fifth. She equaled one world's record and lowered two track records in the process. With a scored start she won a two-and-a-half-furlong race in 27.2 seconds and ran a quarter in 22 flat, carrying 114 pounds.

She had demonstrated one thing in Mexico; she could run brilliantly at the shorter distances. She was a sprinter with rare speed. Bob Kleberg had bred her for great speed. She was not supposed to run farther than three-fourths of a mile and win in good company.[1] She was never tried seriously beyond four and a half furlongs. Her future stretched before her on the short tracks of the Southwest.

One bright summer day in 1945 Ernest Lane paid a visit to the ranch and Bob Kleberg. The upshot of the visit was that Miss Princess was turned over to Lane, who was given one special mission in life: to see that Miss Princess beat Shue Fly.[2]

Miss Princess went to Del Rio, Texas, in May, 1946, for the annual race meet. There she had little competition. On May 17 she beat Vandy and Wee Tot, running an easy 440 yards in 22.4 seconds. On May 19 she repeated her performance against a better field, beating out Rosedale and Vandy and taking the Del Rio Derby in 22.4 seconds. Miss Princess went

[1] Letter dated March 9, 1948, Denhardt Files, King Ranch Folder No. 3.

[2] I first saw Miss Princess in 1945. At that time I was working for and with J. B. Ferguson and Jack Hutchins, and we were running Skippy, Mae West, Jimmy, and Rosedale. We moved down to Skidmore, Texas, to train for some races we had matched with Blondie. Ernest Lane and Miss Princess were there, and, having heard rumors about her, I looked her over carefully. At first glance she didn't reveal her latent short speed. She stood about fourteen–two and a half hands high and weighed about 950 pounds. Her coat was a beautiful medium sorrel, and her most distinguishing mark was a rather small oblong star just above the line of her eyes. She was so smoothly muscled that her power was lost on you. It was not until you studied her stifle, thigh, and gaskin, the depth through the heart, and the muscles over her back, inside her legs, and under her belly that you could recognize the presence of a tremendous running machine. She had one outstanding characteristic that any race-horse man notices immediately, and that was her lovable disposition. Even when wound up tight, she was still as gentle and friendly as a kitten. The next day she ran a 220 against George Parr's Danger Boy. After I saw that race, Miss Princess had gained one more admirer.

174

to Del Rio again for the October meet, and then she proved beyond doubt that she was championship material. Before a record-breaking crowd she gave a preview of what she was to do the following year to Shue Fly. The feature race of that meet was named in honor of General Wainwright, who was on hand to see it run. Entered were Miss Princess; Blondie, a stout-hearted daughter of a great sire, Jimmy Allred; Danger Boy, a brilliant young stallion owned by George Parr; and Mae West, a Louisiana-bred mare belonging to John Ferguson. In that race you could have covered the three mares and a stallion with a blanket, but Miss Princess had what it took to bring home the $11,000.

Several days after that race Miss Princess was taken to Eagle Pass for her last meet of 1946. There she won the open 330-yard race and equaled the world's record of 17.4 seconds doing it. On the last day of the meet she won the Eagle Pass Derby of 440 yards in 22.5 seconds. All in all, it was a satisfactory year for Miss Princess.

The hour that Bob Kleberg and Ernest Lane had been waiting for came almost sooner than they expected. Elmer Hepler never was one to shy from a good race, and with Shue Fly he did not have to. Probably no mare ever lived that ran more races under more trying circumstances than Shue Fly had to run, and she never dodged any contender for her throne. Year after year she had been beating challengers whenever they asked, wherever they were. No horse could have run as many races as she did without being de-feated once in a while, but let it be said to her credit that until Miss Princess appeared on the scene Shue Fly always ran again and beat the horse that had beaten her and so proved that she was the best. To make a long story short, Shue Fly came to Del Rio in May, 1947, to see what all the talk was about concerning this Miss Princess.

The stands were packed to overloading, and a purse of $30,000 awaited the winner. On May 4, the appointed day, the horses went to the gate promptly. For the first time the Del Rio track was laned so that each mare would have a fair run and no interference. Shue Fly, who was exercised more than Miss Princess, cut up in the gate, delaying the start. When the gate was finally sprung, Miss Princess was out first by a nose. At the eighth pole Miss Princess had Shue Fly but only by a neck. At the 300-yard marker Miss

175

Princess made her bid, and the race was no longer in question. Shue Fly, always a great mare, ran the 440 in a little better than 22.5 seconds, fast enough to beat any living horse but Miss Princess, who ran it that day in world-record time, 22.3 seconds for the standing-start quarter. Pat Castile, who rode Miss Princess, said that the race never gave him a worry after the horses broke. Both he and Earl Southern, who rode Shue Fly, weighed in at 111 pounds. Bob Kleberg came to see that race, even though his Thorough-bred Assault, Miss Princess's half brother, was running an important race back east. Wild horses could not have kept that Texan home when that race was run.

August 31, 1947, was the worst day in Miss Princess's life. That was the day John Ferguson's Mae West beat her at Cuero, Texas. The race was not exactly at her distance—350 yards—especially when it was run in the sensational time of 17.5. On September 6, however, Miss Princess had her revenge on Mae West. They broke out of the Cuero starting gate, going 440 yards for a purse of $10,000. Miss Princess began to roll at the 300-yard marker, and Mae was unable to stand the pace. At the 400-yard marker Miss Princess had Mae West, and the outcome was only a matter of time—and what time! The watches showed 22 seconds flat. The track is somewhat downhill, and there was a tail wind. That was the race that Ernest Lane says gave him the greatest thrill and the one in which he thinks Miss Princess ran her best race. Johnny Ferguson thought that Miss Princess's race with Bar-bra B was her best, an opinion shared by Miss Princess's trainer, Paul Simar.

In some ways almost as much excitement was created over the Miss Princess–Barbra B race as over the Shue Fly encounter. That little argument for Miss Princess was also run at Del Rio. Barbra B was the short-horse sensation of 1947—until she met Miss Princess. Barbra deserved her repu-tation. Not only had she beaten C. S. Howard's Thoroughbred Fair Truckle, who had caught the public eye, but—what was more important to short-horsemen—she was setting new track records, something she had not had to do when she beat Fair Truckle. She ran Princess in Del Rio on October 26, 1947. Both horses carried 115 pounds, Tony Licata riding Barbra and Pat Castile, Miss Princess. Miss Princess outbroke Barbra B and was a length on top at the 350 marker and had daylight at the finish. In that race Miss

Princess set a new world's record of 18 seconds flat for 350 yards and a new world's record of 22.2 seconds for the quarter mile—two records in one race, no mean feat.

After the Barbra B race there was really no likely challenger to meet Miss Princess. A few felt that Miss Bank had a chance to win the championship from her. Two stallions, B Seven and Pelican, were occasionally mentioned as possible adversaries. There was nothing for Ernest Lane to do but take Miss Princess to Tucson in February, 1948, and enter the World Championship 440. B Seven was no longer running well, and in the end the field was composed of Miss Princess, Miss Bank, and Pelican. Miss Princess was assigned 124 pounds; Miss Bank, 112; and Pelican, 114. Miss Bank broke on top for the first 100 yards. Miss Princess, after what was for her a slow start, rapidly picked up speed and gradually overtook Miss Bank, to win in 22.3 seconds. She was now the undisputed owner of the title World's Champion Quarter Running Horse. Like her half brother Assault, she had come to the top of her class, but, unlike him, there was no one on the horizon to threaten her. Bob Kleberg had avenged Shue Fly's defeat of Nobody's Friend and had produced the fastest running mare of her day. After her days of glory she returned to the ranch and became a brood mare.

28. Show Horses and Loyd Jinkens

BOB KLEBERG was faced with something of a dilemma when it was suggested that he show the King Ranch Quarter Horses. The ranch had always shown a few horses at neighboring towns to support the efforts of the communities involved, but never as a serious attempt to put out a show string. Normally, the primary reason for showing animals is to advertise one's stock and attract buyers. The King Ranch was not particularly concerned with attracting buyers for its horses; the owners bred for their own use and could sell without trouble any surplus they might have. Nevertheless, Bob Kleberg's friends kept telling him that his sorrel horses were so good that in all fairness to the breed association and to the public he should exhibit their quality and ability.

Another factor that deterred Kleberg from showing the ranch horses was his conviction that he could not afford to send any of his trusted associates, such as Dr. Northway or Lauro Cavazos, on the show circuit. He needed them on the ranch. On the other hand, he could not afford to let anyone but a top man take the horses, since show horses must be fitted and shown properly. Moreover, Kleberg wanted the horses entered in performance classes as well as in conformation classes. The performance class that is considered the best indication of cow-horse ability is the cutting-horse class. Kleberg would have to have a top man in that field to show his horses to best advantage. For a few years George Clegg had been showing and racing ranch

178

horses, but George's greatest interest was in racing. If the King Ranch horses were to be shown the way Bob Kleberg wanted them shown, a top-notch man had to be found who could both fit a horse for conformation shows and ride one in performance classes. Loyd Jinkens seemed the ideal person to fulfill those requirements.

Loyd Jinkens (whose name is sometimes incorrectly spelled Lloyd Jenkins) was born in Nolan County, Texas, before World War I, in the home of his mother's parents, Mr. and Mrs. J. M. Bryson. The Brysons were pioneer settlers in the area, and Loyd came from sturdy stock on both sides of his family. His father, T. C. Jinkens, was one of the first ranchers in Nolan County, and young Loyd helped his father drive cattle to the shipping point in Sweetwater. The drive, of about thirty miles, must have seemed a long way to the young Jinkens and to his little sorrel pony, Dolly. Loyd grew up hearing about horses and cattle, grass and water (still the basic ingredients of the talk of all real stockmen).

Horses had always been important to the Jinkens family. When the drought of 1917 hit, the Jinkenses rounded up about seventy-five horses and drove them to market in Fort Worth, almost two hundred miles east, to sell them for the cash necessary to see the family through the dry spell.

Loyd's first job as a cowboy was on an uncle's ranch in Runnels County. He stayed there for several years and then moved to Tarrant County, to another ranch owned by the same uncle, S. H. McNay. He stayed with the McNays and today lives on a part of the original McNay ranch. As the McNays grew older, Loyd bought land from them and managed their cow outfit. In 1929, Loyd married Lena Bonds, a beautiful young schoolteacher he met in Nolan County.

During World War I, Loyd's father had sold a number of horses to the Remount Service, as well as some pack mules he had raised and trained. From childhood Loyd had assisted his father with the horses and had begun breaking them when he was twelve. He entered his first cutting-horse contest in 1933 and immediately attracted attention. He was recognized as a real sportsman with a special talent for riding and training cutting horses. He trained and rode Red Boy to win the first National Cutting Horse Championship. He was instrumental in organizing the Cutting Horse Association and

179

would become its president in 1953. Over the years he has won hundreds of medals and many dollars in cutting contests.

Loyd first made headlines in the Quarter Horse world in 1944, when he bought Peppy's Pepper, a son of Peppy P-212, from the King Ranch. Two years later he sold the stallion to Dan Fowley, of Dallas, for $26,500, by far the highest price paid for a Quarter Horse up to that time. In 1947 and 1948 he showed his cutting horses at the Chicago International Livestock Show and made national headlines in 1948 by stopping a heifer that jumped the fence and found herself in the audience.

After the American Quarter Horse Association was organized in 1940, he became interested in Quarter Horses and showed a few. At that time, though, he was still best known for his success with cutting horses.

Bob Kleberg had heard about Loyd's ability to get the most out of horses, and eventually he decided to have Loyd take some of the better ranch animals to show and work in contests. He invited Loyd to the ranch, and a string of animals was picked out for him. The arrangement was continued full time from 1949 to 1962. While touring the country showing King Ranch horses, Loyd won 383 blue ribbons and 99 purple ones. He also had 84 reserve champions. In all, Jinkens won almost 2,000 trophies, including ribbons, cups, saddles, blankets, and bridles.

Probably the best show horse Loyd worked with was Hired Hand, a horse that, unlike many show winners, was even greater in the stud than in the show ring or performance arena. Hired Hand's full brother Little Man was shown at the same time, and he too was a consistent winner. At the State Fair in Dallas in 1948, Hired Hand won Grand Champion, and Little Man won the reserve trophy. Hired Hand was the better of the two, not only in conformation but also in cutting. Both were excellent enough to distance all other competitors.[1]

Two other King Ranch stallions shown by Loyd won grand and reserve championships at Dallas in 1951. The horses were owned by Sumner Pingree, of Cuba, but were shown by Loyd at Bob Kleberg's request.[2] They were

1 Letter dated October 29, 1968, Denhardt Files, Loyd Jinkens Folder.
2 For more about Sumner Pingree, see Chapters 30 and 31.

Cuban Brown (Rey del Poblano) and Cuban Red (Hi Jo del Rey). The former won the grand, and the latter the reserve, championship. Both were by Rey del Rancho. Cuban Brown was out of an outcross mare sired by the Thoroughbred Sudden Change, and Cuban Red was out of a daughter of the great High Gear by the Old Sorrel. Loyd kept and showed the two stallions for several years with great success.

Anita Chica was the best of the many outstanding mares shown by Loyd. Anita was registered P-76,322. A bay, she was foaled in 1956. Her sire was Rey del Rancho. Her dam was La Anita, a bay mare born in 1940 by Tomate Laureles and out of a Little Richard mare. Anita Chica is ranch-bred, and all her ancestors dating back fifty-two years were also ranch-bred. Loyd showed her from the summer of 1957 to the fall of 1962. She won one Champion of Champions award, forty-one Grand Champion awards, fifteen Reserve Champion awards, and sixty blue ribbons. Like Hired Hand, she was a top performer in cutting-horse contests.

In the shows Loyd was assisted by his brother T. C. Jinkens, Jr., and by his daughter, Margaret, now Mrs. Fred T. Slocum, of Brady, Texas. Margaret is particularly proud (as is Loyd) of her work with Hired Hand's Cardinal, whom she helped break and train and whom she rode in many of his wins in cutting-horse contests. T. C. joined Loyd when he was discharged from the service after World War II, and the brothers still work together, T. C. being particularly active in training, as well as in showing.

After 1962, Jinkens became less active in the show and performance rings. He needed to devote more time to his own interests, and Bob Kleberg believed that the ranch had pretty well shown its wares. Loyd's own Quarter Horses, usually numbering around fifty brood mares and about fifty more stallions, geldings, and colts, are predominantly of King Ranch breeding. His principal stallion, Socks Five, a grandson of Wimpy P-1, is a beautiful individual.

At the time of this writing, the King Ranch has no large-scale show program, though some of its horses are still shown on occasion as a courtesy or favor to friends and associates.

SOME KING RANCH CHAMPIONS

Bill Cody, by Wimpy P-1:
    Eleventh Leading Sire of AQHA Champions
    Fourteenth Leading Sire of ROM Qualifiers

Wimpy II, by Wimpy P-1:
    Seventh Leading Maternal Grandsire of AQHA Champions (tied)
    Twentieth Leading Sire of AQHA Champions
    Sixteenth Leading Sire of ROM Qualifiers
    Sire of Annie Wade, 5th leading dam of AQHA Champions

Showdown, by Wimpy P-1:
    Ninth Leading Sire of AQHA Champions

Silver Wimpy, by Wimpy P-1:
    Seventh Leading Maternal Grandsire of AQHA Champions (tied)

Pep Up, by Peppy P-212:
    Sire of Shady Dell, Leading Dam of AQHA Champions
    Tenth leading Maternal Grandsire of AQHA Champions

H. H. Dee, by Hired Hand P-2495:
    Fourth leading Produce of Dam Class Winner for 1966

Rey del Rancho, by Ranchero P-215:
    Sire of Anita Chica, Champion of Champions, 41 Grand Championships

The King Ranch is fourth leading breeder of ROM Qualifiers; sixth leading breeder of AQHA Champions; sixth leading breeder of 1966 Performance Class Winners; tenth leading breeder of 1966 Halter Class Winners (most wins); twelfth leading breeder of Performance Point Earners.

29. Performance Horses

THE King Ranch is one of the top four breeders of performance horses in the nation, in spite of the fact that the ranch keeps all its best horses on the ranch. In spite of the ranch policy of retaining the best, the colts that have reached buyers have set records as performing horses. They are the horses to beat when Quarter Horse contests are held, whether in cutting, roping, racing, or other performance tests.

The reason for the success of the King Ranch horses is not hard to find: it is the demanding tests that all of the breeding stock has had to pass, generation after generation, back to Old Sorrel. Almost fifty years of selecting and breeding only superior performing horses to superior performing horses have produced today's King Ranch horses. No other strain of Quarter Horses has been maintained for so long—dating back to twenty years before the Quarter Horse Association was organized.

Watching the fillies and colts being tested on the ranch is a delightful experience. Let us say that you leave early in the morning (as I did one day in 1968) and drive about twenty-five miles southwest across the ranch, past groups of dark cherry-red Santa Gertrudis cattle and bands of sorrel brood mares and colts grazing or standing around a water hole. You pass through a group of oil wells unobtrusively going about their business, looking a little out of place in the grass- and brushland of the ranch. Finally, after encountering wild turkeys, bobwhites, white-tailed deer, and perhaps a few wary javelinas, you come to a large opening where several hundred Santa Gertrudis cattle are being circled by a few Kineños. Around the chuck wagon parked in the mesquite to one side are other *vaqueros,* drinking coffee and waiting for the *patrón*'s arrival. One thing sure to strike you about the picture is the quality of the horses the Kineños are riding. Tied to mesquite and patches of brush near the men is as uniform and excellent a group of cow horses as you are ever likely to see. Averaging about fifteen hands high, they are clean-legged, deep-chested, and good-headed, with eyes and ears that miss nothing. You may also notice, tied to the wheels of the wagon, two young stallions. They are not saddled, but they soon will be, for today they are on trial.

As you arrive, there is an outbreak of conversation, all in Spanish, between the *vaqueros* and the man for whom they have been waiting, Dick Kleberg. Someone takes Dick's saddle out of the trunk of the car and prepares to saddle the colt Dick plans to ride. While the horses are being readied, more coffee is served, and the grass and the weather are discussed. When Dick puts down his cup, that is the signal for everyone to rise and mount his horse. Dick swings up on one colt, the foreman on the other. They ride out slowly toward the herd, the colts beautifully behaved but still showing the interest young horses have in everything that moves in front of or around them. Like most high-spirited colts, these two have a tendency to overreact. Dick rides easily, his body following the sudden movements of the colt—subconsciously, for Dick's mind is on the questions he is asking and the answers he is getting from his foreman. His full attention will be on the colt, however, when the action starts.

The riders stop a short distance from the herd to continue the conversation. Although it is only about eight o'clock, the air is already getting warm and seems heavy. Dick beckons to you and takes you to a low mesquite to show you the stick nest of a paisano. One seldom sees a roadrunner's nest; it is usually too well hidden.

As you return to the herd, you notice that a couple of older cows have made a break for the brush. Two *vaqueros* ride after them with the abandon of Comanches, and the cattle are returned to the herd. Now Dick and the foreman ride into the closely grouped cattle. The colt Dick is riding seems

184

to sense what is about to happen. He seems to be stalking the herd, open to the slightest suggestion from his rider. He follows his rider's cues while his eyes and ears search for the animal his rider wants. Somehow he knows which one has been chosen before you do—and you were watching every move.

Now, quietly, the colt moves through the restless cattle, working the chosen animal, a heifer, to one side of the herd. There is no trouble until the heifer finds herself at the edge. Then she breaks into a lope and tries to get back around the colt and into the security of the group. But the colt was expecting this and is waiting for her. Each turn she takes, he is with her, head always toward her. Finally she finds herself alone and a little distance from the herd. She is picked up by two of the *vaqueros*. Dick turns the colt and makes him walk quietly back into the herd for another selection.

Such tests as this one have been carried out on the ranch since 1918. All the colts, and the fillies as well, are expected to perform in such fashion and are allowed only minor mistakes. If the colt is not to be gelded, he must prove himself outstanding. Perhaps he will show special skill in roping tests or speed tests. If not, he will spend his life as a gelding on the ranch, doing that for which he was bred, working cattle.

Unfortunately, the public never gets a chance to see the cow horses at work on the ranch. In its operations the ranch uses about two thousand horses, a large percentage of which are top individuals. To meet so heavy a demand continues to be the primary purpose of the breeding program. The ranch always has first choice of all the young stock; some of the others are sold. The latter are the only ones the public has a chance to observe at work.

Today the American Quarter Horse Association keeps records of the performance of horses at approved shows. It awards prizes to the winners and publishes statistics on performance horses. The records of the Quarter Horse Association reveal how the King Ranch horses who have gone out into the world of competition have fared. The following official statistics were published in the *Quarter Horse Journal* in May, 1968.

Among the leading sires of Point Earning Performance Horses were (1) Joe Cody by Bill Cody with fourteen get gathering 148½ points, (2) Showdown by Wimpy with twelve get gathering 132½ points, and (3) Wimpy III

185

by Wimpy II with eleven get gathering 45½ points. Two King Ranch stallions were also listed in the top twenty Leading Sires of Show Register of Merit Qualifiers: Wimpy II by Wimpy with twenty-five qualifiers and eight AQHA champions and Bill Cody by Wimpy with twenty-eight qualifiers and eleven AQHA champions.

Joe Cody by Bill Cody stood twelfth in the list of leading sires of 1967 Show Register of Merit Qualifiers with four get qualifying in 1967 for a total of fifteen, and he also had three AQHA champions.

The King Ranch is also in the top ten Leading Breeders of 1967 Performance Point Earners. The ranch had fourteen point earners, who gained 78 points. Nine of them won twenty-six shows, which is a pretty good record.

Showdown by Wimpy and Socks Five by Silver Wimpy together sired thirty class winners in 1967. Between them they won 134 classes.

The most respected classification—and the one all breeders would like to make—is the Leading Breeders of Register of Merit Horses. Considering the hundreds of breeders in each state who enter thousands of horses in contests every year, one can see that this group comprises a select and exclusive circle. A small handful of breeders (including the King Ranch) is found high on this list every year, year after year. In 1967 the King Ranch was listed fourth. Besides the ranch, the group always at or near the top is made up of Waggoners, the Burnetts, and the Wiescamps. King Ranch blood has produced forty-eight qualifiers and fifteen AQHA champions. They are sixth in the list of Leading Breeders of AQHA Champions.

When the list of Leading Sires of AQHA Champions is examined, the King Ranch is found to be responsible for four of the top twenty-five stallions: Showdown, Bill Cody, Wimpy II, and Wimpy III, who altogether have produced forty-one AQHA champions. The ranch is also responsible for four of the top eighteen Leading Maternal Grandsires of AQHA Champions, accounting for thirty-seven AQHA champions. King Ranch breeding also placed three dams in the first eight Leading Dams of AQHA Champions.

When one bears in mind that the ranch does not breed to sell, show, or contest its horses, and that only those that leave the ranch at the annual sale or as gifts ever contest, the record becomes all the more amazing. In the years when the ranch allowed George Clegg and Loyd Jinkens to show a few animals, the Quarter Horse Association had not yet begun to keep its present complex records. Most breeders contest and show their animals to advertise their establishments and increase sales. The ranch has no need to advertise. And yet, despite the fact that no serious attempt has ever been made to select the best King Ranch horses and train them for the Quarter Horse shows, the record is outstanding.

30. Sales

ALTHOUGH the purpose of the Quarter Horse breeding program on the King Ranch has always been providing the ranch with working cow horses, the excellent reputation the horses early established soon brought many prospective buyers to the ranch. It proved very difficult to turn down friends and friends of friends. To accommodate such persons, many horses had to be sold or given away.

In the beginning the requests were more or less moderate and did not present a serious problem. As the King Ranch horses began to appear in the various shows and contests across the country, however, their ability and unique characteristics attracted wide attention. Loyd Jinkens's show string was another important factor in creating public interest. Detailed records of the early Quarter Horse sales are not available, but, as an example, in 1944 at least seven King Ranch Quarter Horses were sold to buyers from Oklahoma, Montana, Kansas, California, Louisiana, and Mexico. This figure probably does not represent total sales and also does not include gift animals. No sales records are available for 1945. In 1946 incomplete records show that at least thirteen horses were sold to Texans. In the same year three ranch Quarter Horses went to California, three to Oklahoma, one to Colorado, and one to Nevada. By 1948 so many requests were coming in and so many buyers were showing up at the ranch that some formal arrangement had to be made to dispose of salable stock. In that year twenty-four buyers from

188

different sections of the country bought thirty colts and eight fillies worth $19,600. To complicate things further, it seemed that for each buyer there were ten lookers who wanted to see all the horses. Bob Kleberg came to the decision that the best solution was to hold an annual sale to which the steady stream of buyers could be invited. The annual sale also solved the problem of maintaining a year-round staff of men to gather and show horses.

On November 10, 1950, the first annual sale was held. Everything possible was done to ensure a successful sale. Henry (Hank) Wiescamp, of Alamosa, Colorado, was employed as auctioneer.[1] Representatives of the major livestock magazines, such as the *Quarter Horse Journal, Cattleman, Western Horseman,* and the *Western Livestock Journal,* were invited to attend.

The highest bidder at the first sale was Louis P. Reed, of Meridian, Texas, who paid $3,200 for a colt by Wimpy and out of La Maca (Macanudo-Verganza). The biggest buyer, however, was Sumner Pingree, of Cuba, who was stocking his ranch with Santa Gertrudis cattle and wanted King Ranch Quarter Horses to work them. He asked Loyd Jinkens to help him select the horses. He paid $4,000 for two Rey del Rancho colts, one out of China Poblana (Sudden Change–Martina) and the other out of Coquena (Old Sorrel–High Gear). C. K. Russom, of Fort Worth, bought a Hired Hand colt for $2,200 and another colt for $1,000, as well as a filly. In all, fifty-one horses were sold for a total of $33,440. The average price was $655.69.

On November 10, 1951, the second annual sale was held. That year seventeen colts and fillies went for $1,000 or more each, the top price being $3,755. Again Sumner Pingree was the biggest buyer. He paid the top price for a Hired Hand filly out of Pep Americana (Peppy-Americana). He also bought three others for over $1,000 apiece: $1,800 for a Hired Hand filly, $1,500 for a Chamaco colt who was out of Coquena (Old Sorrel–High Gear), and $1,300 for a filly by Caracol. In all he bought five fillies and a colt. Two other big buyers were D. M. Cogdell, of Snyder, Texas, who also bought five fillies and a colt. In point of numbers Ringling Brothers, Barnum and Bailey Circus bought the most horses that year, purchasing twelve colts for

---

[1] Walter Britton, of College Station, Texas, assisted Hank in the first and second sales. In the third he replaced Hank as principal auctioneer and has held that post ever since.

$5,990. The twenty-three fillies sold at the second sale averaged $1,029.56 each; the thirty-four colts, $804. The over-all average was $895, about one-third better than the year before.

The next year, 1952, saw the first major policy change with regard to the annual sales. The ranch could not afford to sell too much of its breeding stock, and it was decided to limit the number of colts and fillies to be sold each year to twenty-five.

In 1952, Sumner Pingree topped the sale when he bought a Wimpy filly out of Muneca Peppy (Peppy–mare by Solis) and another out of La Loca (Macunado–China Chiquita), for $3,000 each. The second-largest buyer was Robert Manziel, of Tyler, Texas. He paid $1,000 for a gray filly by Wimpy's Greylake and out of Spokane Rose. He also paid $790 for a black colt by Dos de Oros, and $750 for a brown filly by Saltillo Jr. Robert S. Lard, of Fort Worth, paid $1,500 for a Wimpy colt, and Patrick Lambert, of Refugio, Texas, paid the same amount for a colt by Rey del Rancho. The horses sold for an average price of $965.80.

At the fourth annual sale, held on November 10, 1953, the highest bid was only $1,450, but six horses sold for $1,000 or more each. The high colt was by Pretty Buck out of a mare the ranch had purchased in foal. He was purchased by Bill Reynal, of Argentina. Patrick Lambert, of Refugio, paid $1,200 for a filly by Hired Hand and out of La Chusa. Bert Fields, of Dallas, paid the same price for a Hired Hand filly.

The fifth and sixth sales were held on November 10, 1954 and 1955. The high price for the 1955 sale was $2,200, paid by Ed Porath, of Northview, Michigan, for a Hired Hand II filly out of Graviella Chiquita. He also bought a Hired Hand colt for $2,000. By 1955 the sale average was up to $1,358.

The 1957 sale represented a departure. Instead of a winter sale in November, it was decided to hold the sale in April. 1957 proved to be one of the best years; only two horses went for less than $1,000. Ed Porath was once again the biggest buyer. He paid $4,000 for a Hired Hand's Cardinal filly out of Pimientomate (Little Man–mare by Tomate Laureles) and $3,550 for a Hired Hand II colt out of Golandrina (Peppy Compania). The 1957 sale average was $1,571.

190

During the next three years the sale average increased almost exactly $1,000 a year. In 1958 the average was $2,084; in 1959, $3,036; in 1960, $3,991. The biggest buyer in those years was Frank Daugherty, of Olton, Texas. In 1958 he paid $3,400 for a Wimpy Jr. colt out of Espeja Martina, and in 1959 he topped the sale when he bought a Hired Hand's Cardinal colt out of Vibora Tres for $4,650. In 1959, Perry Shankle, of San Antonio, paid $4,150 for a filly by Hired Hand, and C. N. Cooke, of Corpus Christi, paid $4,050 for another Hired Hand filly.

In the 1960 sale Daugherty bought a Wimpy Jr. colt out of Almendra (Peppy–Dollie Chiquita) for $6,600. The high figure at that sale was the $7,000 paid by W. B. Blakemore, of Midland, Texas, for a Hired Hand colt out of Patos Blancas de Javiel. Only two colts sold for less than $2,000, and they were not under that figure by very much. This amount compares very favorably with the first sale, when twenty-one of the sale colts and fillies went for less than $500 each.

After 1960 the sales leveled out, and the rapid increase in prices halted, in line with industry-wide trends. Nevertheless, the sale held on April 18, 1968, was one of the best on record. The highest-priced individual was a filly by El Nino and out of La Alejandra. She was sold to the Hualalai Ranch of Honolulu for $5,000. The second-highest price was paid for a colt by El Rey Rojo, out of Wylie's Pearl, who was sold to Don Corley, of Fort Worth, for $4,650. Other colts went for $4,500 and $4,375. The second-highest price for a filly was $3,000, paid by the Paisano Ranch of Corpus Christi for a Socks Five filly out of Rojo's Lady. Sale total for the twenty-five colts was $57,235, and the average price was $2,289 (the fillies averaged $451 more than the colts).[2]

All in all, the sales have proved an effective way for the ranch to sell its surplus horses and allow the public access to the reserve of good blood maintained by the ranch.

2 For more information on the sales, see Appendix 7. Most of the information for this chapter was taken from marked sales programs on file at the King Ranch, and the figures were checked by Gail Boon, of the office staff, who is the Quarter Horse specialist.

31. Expansion

Today the King Ranch is considerably changed from the cow camp Richard King set up on Santa Gertrudis Creek in 1854. It is now a modern business corporation with divisions scattered across the United States and around the world. Year by year the ranch continues to grow.

Though the activities of the King Ranch could not have been termed paltry under Captain King or the elder Kleberg, in the early days it was a relatively simple operation compared with the worldwide enterprise developed under Robert J. Kleberg, Jr. Many lesser men would have sat back and enjoyed the fruits of so great an accomplishment. After all, the ranch had developed the first new breed of cattle in the New World, as well as a special strain of American Quarter Horses. Furthermore, the ranch had set the Thoroughbred industry on its ear by producing two Kentucky Derby winners, a triple-crown winner, and a horse that won more money than any that had come before it. Certainly no other ranch, and no other man, had done so much—"as a breeding thing."[1]

King Ranch lands outside Texas tell only a fraction of the story. Expanded interest in all the critical factors that go into beef production and pasture utilization are manifest in all lands owned or controlled by the ranch.

[1] Bob Kleberg said, "At the start I didn't know if I was going into racing or not—but if I was [it would be] something to show what the ranch could do as a breeding thing." Lea, *The King Ranch*, II, 670.

192

New methods and new machinery have been developed as needed. Perhaps, indeed, the ranch's greatest advantage has been ownership of hundreds of thousands of acres, which meant that equipment could be designed and built for specialized jobs, such as clearing brush. Problems of water usage and conservation, land clearance, pasture grass, roads, fences, corrals, and marketing—and all the other myriad problems surrounding cattle production—have been met head on, with enough brains, energy, and financing to solve them as they arose.

Other concerns than grass and cattle have been pursued on the King Ranch. For example, a wildlife department is maintained by the ranch with specialists who carry on the work of preserving and improving not only the native game birds and animals but also exotic imports from other parts of the world. The ranch requested, and the state of Texas agreed, that thousands of acres of the ranch be designated a game preserve. The result has been that bobwhites, turkeys, doves, deer, javelinas, and other game have increased inside King Ranch fences while declining elsewhere.

Other valuables lie under King Ranch soil. In 1933 the ranch signed a lease with Humble Oil and Refining Company. Within twenty years there were 650 producing oil and gas wells on King Ranch lands. Strict though amicable control of oil-production methods by the Klebergs has resulted in the elimination of the unsightly accouterments visible on lands owned by ranchers blessed with less foresight. Consequently, the debris around other successful oil fields is never in sight. As one rides across the ranch, one is scarcely aware of the discreet pumps, neat pipelines, and unobtrusive storage depots surrounded by green grass, cattle, horses, mesquite, and wildlife. The refineries have been a little more difficult to camouflage, but the ranch is working on the problem.

Petroleum development made some changes on the ranch, in rather unsuspected ways. In the days before oil was discovered, one could go through a gate, set his directions, and ride until he came to the next fence, ten or fifteen miles away. The oil industry needed direct transportation, and heavy equipment necessitated paved or all-weather roads. As a result, today there are more than four hundred miles of improved roads on the King Ranch, with regular road crews who spend all their time maintaining them. For the most

193

part, cattle drives are a thing of the past, and long horseback rides to staging areas are infrequent. Living in isolated cow camps for days at a time is also ended. Mobile camps, transported by trucks, meet cow horses and cowboys (who also arrive on wheels) at the holding area.

When the ranch began to obtain pasturelands outside Texas, the development was no surprise to those aware of the tremendous energy of the Klebergs. Expansion was inevitable—it was only a question of timing. In the beginning expansion was triggered by changing market conditions. For many years the ranch ran steers in Oklahoma and Kansas, primarily to conserve the home pastures for cows and calves during the dry summer months. By 1946, Bob Kleberg had realized that changing demands dictated a move nearer the market in order to realize a reasonable profit. The first land purchase outside Texas was a range of about ten thousand acres near Coatsville, Pennsylvania. On that division, called the Buck and Doe Run Valley Farms, about five thousand steers are matured for the market each year and delivered by truck in a few hours to the best market, Baltimore, Philadelphia, or New York.

Soon thereafter a small ranch (if one can call more than one section of bluegrass country near Lexington, Kentucky, a "small ranch") was obtained. This division, set up in 1946–47, was to serve a twofold purpose. It would concentrate on horse breeding but would also serve as a haven for a small herd of selected purebred Santa Gertrudis, to be kept there as insurance in the event that an outbreak of hoof-and-mouth disease in Mexico should sweep across the border, making it necessary to destroy the ranch herd. The Kentucky division also acted as a show window for eastern visitors of the outstanding features of the Santa Gertrudis cattle and the ranch horses.

Expansion overseas, which came later, was a logical development of ranch interests. For years Latin Americans had been visiting the ranch and admiring the cattle and horses. When one recalls the close association the ranch had always had with Spanish-speaking employees and friends south of the border—and the fact that Spanish is really the language of the ranch —the number of visitors from Central and South America is not surprising. What is surprising is that so many came from other regions of the world.

Many foreign visitors were not satisfied with seeing the stock but were

194

Richard M. Kleberg, Jr., cutting yearlings on the Laureles Division on a King Ranch Quarter Horse.

Robert J. Kleberg, Jr., president of the King Ranch. He is the person most responsible for its expansion, as well as for the development of the Santa Gertrudis cattle and sorrel Quarter Horses.

Richard M. Kleberg, Sr. He was the older brother of Robert J. Kleberg, Jr., and the father of Richard M. Kleberg, Jr. He was active in all ranch activities until his death in 1955.

Caesar Kleberg on the porch of his Norias Division residence. He was the cousin of Robert J. Kleberg, Jr., and Richard M. Kleberg, Sr. It was he who purchased the Old Sorrel from George Clegg. He died in 1946.

George Clegg was a famous Quarter Horse breeder of Alice, Texas. He sold the King Ranch many horses, and he bred the Old Sorrel and owned Hickory Bill. He died in 1959.

Ott Adams was one of the greatest Quarter Horse breeders of all time. He lived near Alfred, Texas. Little Joe was his greatest stallion. He furnished many horses to the King Ranch at the outset of the Quarter Horse program. He died in 1963.

Dr. J. K. Northway, the internationally known veterinarian of the King Ranch, went to work for the ranch in 1916 and has been there ever since. He has been a key figure in all of Bob Kleberg's livestock activities. No one outside the Kleberg family has been more closely connected with the development of the Santa Gertrudis cattle and the sorrel Quarter Horse.

John W. Dial brought Chicaro to Texas from Louisiana and sold him, along with some great Little Joe mares, to Bob Kleberg. He was a horseman who raised and raced both Thoroughbreds and Quarter Horses. He died in 1967.

John W. Almond knows as much as any living man about the Quarter Horses of South Texas. For fifty years he has been a horseman interested in both Quarter Horses and Thoroughbreds. In his younger days he did a lot of roping as well. He sold many mares to the King Ranch.

Ernest Lane raced many King Ranch horses for Bob Kleberg. He is especially remembered for his handling of Miss Princess, whom he campaigned to the World's Championship. He lived at Odem, Texas, until his recent death.

Loyd Jinkens had great success showing the King Ranch Quarter Horses, among them Hired Hand (whom he is riding in the picture) and Anita Chica. He lives and ranches near Fort Worth, Texas.

King Ranch brands as carried in the *Corpus Christi Advertiser* in 1872.

The Jockey Club,

CERTIFICATE OF FOAL REGISTRATION.

1901.

For racing purposes only.

This is to certify that the Bay Filly named *Lucretia M.* by *The Hero* out of *Bird* foaled March 17 1901 is duly registered by The Jockey Club.

Marks: Star x

_____

_____

_____

F. K. Sturgis.
Secretary.

James E. Wheeler
Registrar.

Issued to Samuel Watkins.

New York Sept 13th 1901

CERTIFICATE TO BE PRESERVED AND TRANSFERRED TO THE PURCHASER IF THIS HORSE IS SOLD.— RECORD TRANSFER ON REVERSE SIDE.

Samuel Watkins.
Little Grove
Stock Farm

Petersburg, Ill. May 10 1901.

Hickory Bill
Dam Lucretia M. ¼ Mile, time 21 sec. ½ Mile, 47 sec. ⅜, 1.02. On Chicago Track as two year old. ⅛ mile Time 10 sec. thereby beating Neverfret. & Neverfret holds World record for half mile 46 sec. Sire Peter McCue ½ Mile Time 47 — ¼ Mile Time 21½ sec. as a two year old.

The registration papers of Hickory Bill and his dam, Lucretia M., sent to George Clegg from Samuel Watkins's stock farm at Petersburg, Illinois. Hickory Bill was the sire of the Old Sorrel.

Richard M. Kleberg, Jr., working cattle on a ranch Quarter Horse.

Kineños at work on the cattle range.

eager purchasers. Cattle and horses that went to countries overseas were so successful in their new homes that they stirred further interest. Many foreign buyers were deterred by the cost of shipping the stock from Texas. It soon became obvious that if the ranch was going to profit from this demand it would have to breed and sell stock in those countries where the interest was greatest, such as Australia, Argentina, Brazil, Colombia, Cuba, Guatemala, Mexico, Peru, Puerto Rico, and Venezuela. It was decided to buy ranches in some of those countries as a test of the program. Perhaps the one consideration that did more than any other to persuade Bob Kleberg to expand the ranch into foreign countries was his desire to maintain the quality and superior characteristics of the sorrel Quarter Horses and the Santa Gertrudis cattle. If there was no control over the breeding and selling of horses and cattle advertised as of King Ranch breeding, inferior individuals could easily destroy the market for ranch stock.

Curiously enough, it was in Australia that the first overseas demand for Santa Gertrudis cattle developed. The Australian government wrote to the ranch inquiring about the possibility of obtaining a bull for experimental breeding purposes. The results were very encouraging, and interest in the breed grew. In 1952, in answer to the demand for more Santa Gertrudis cattle, two companies were formed: a purebred division, located near Warwick, Queensland, and a 240,640-acre ranch for a commercial herd near Clermont, Queensland. Each company included some local cattlemen as stockholders.

The first large shipment to Australia, including 202 heifers and 73 young bulls, was sent from the ranch in May, 1952. Four Quarter Horse stallions were included in the shipment. After incredible confusion, red tape, and bureaucratic snafus (with a dock strike thrown in for good measure) the cattle eventually arrived in Australia. In 1953 a shipment limited to horses —17 colts and 26 mares—left for Australia. Later, 3 more stallions and 9 fillies were sent to supplement the earlier group. Two subsequent shipments included 9 stallions and 17 fillies. In all, by 1966, 43 stallions and mares had arrived down under.

The Quarter Horse proved to be as popular in Australia as the Santa Gertrudis cattle. Bob Kleberg had noticed on an earlier trip that the grade Thoroughbreds in Australia were about on a par with the horses he had in-

195

herited when he took over management of the King Ranch many years before. It didn't take a lot of figuring for him to realize that there was a need, and would soon be a demand, for his horses.

By 1960 so many Australians wanted to buy Quarter Horses that a regular yearly auction was arranged. A few horses had been sold earlier, although no attempt had been made to attract buyers. Today both horse and cattle sales are held in Australia as they are in Texas. The sales are a tremendous success, and animals of King Ranch origin are scattered throughout Australia. The Australian Quarter Horse Association was chartered, in co-operation with the American Quarter Horse Association. Peter Baillieu, a director of King Ranch Australia, was its first president.

For a while Cuba was the site of one of the most active divisions of the overseas King Ranch. Before the revolution the ranch had extensive interests in Camaguey and Oriente provinces. Leading stockmen on the island were developing small herds of Santa Gertrudis and sorrel King Ranch horses, and the demand was increasing for more purebred stock.[2] The Castro regime has changed all of that, however.

In Chapter 30 mention was made of Sumner Pingree's purchases of Quarter Horses from the ranch. All the horses were shipped to his ranch in Cuba, where he used them to work the Santa Gertrudis cattle he had bought. What the situation in Cuba is now is anybody's guess, although it would seem that anything as basic as the livestock industry would be encouraged. No doubt the King Ranch cattle and horses are now owned by the government. It may be that the animals are being bred indiscriminately and are now common individuals. It takes years of selective breeding to create good individuals, who in turn can lose their purity and prepotency by just a few crosses of inferior blood.

In Brazil the King Ranch operates in conjunction with Companhia Swift do Brasil, S.A., a foreign subsidiary of Swift and Company. A large tract of land was purchased in Brazil under the name King Ranch do Brasil, S.A. It is located in the southwest corner of the state of São Paulo, on the Paranapanema River. Both horses and cattle have been sent down to stock

2 The first shipment of Quarter Horses took place in April, 1952, and included eighteen mares and two stallions.

the ranch. The first shipment was made in January, 1954, and included 34 Santa Gertrudis bulls and 225 heifers. In the following month 7 Quarter Horse mares and a stallion followed the cattle to Brazil.[3] Today the ranch has about reached its goal of 60,000 Santa Gertrudis roaming the 147,000 acres, with sorrel King Ranch Quarter Horses working the cattle. In the beginning Quarter Horse stallions were used to give the native Brazilian Crillo horses a little more size and quality. The first senior stallion used was Saltillo Jr., who was by Saltillo by Ranchero. When Saltillo died in 1960, he was replaced by Caracolito, who was by Caracol and out of La Calavaza. Caracolito is a beautiful individual who had a distinguished show record in the United States before he was sent to Brazil. In 1967 the first public sale of King Ranch Quarter Horses was held in Brazil.

The success of the King Ranch overseas ventures is amply shown by the following advertisement carried by the ranch in several national magazines. It opened with the statement that the King Ranch had an interest in 350,000 cattle:

> Yes, that's the correct figure; it surprises us somewhat also when we pause to consider that in the relatively short span of fifteen years we and our partners in the United States and overseas have put together a breeding herd of this size on three continents. The illustration above shows how it is paying off; in the past twelve months alone we have sold over $1,000,000 U.S. in purebred and crossbred Santa Gertrudis bulls and crossbred heifers in Australia. Our properties there are producing at a level that we hope our newer acquisitions will soon reach.
>
> We have shipped nearly 1,700 purebred Santa Gertrudis bulls to our joint venture in Florida, the Big B Ranch, over a three year period and at last feel that it is almost stocked for full production. We still have unfilled commitments for bulls on our properties in Latin America. Our operation in Venezuela is just getting underway and we have acquired, in the past few weeks, an additional 300,000 acres of rain forest in the Amazon basin in Brazil. However, it is in Argentina, one of the top livestock countries in the world where competition between breeds is the keenest, that our need for quality bulls is most pressing. By supplying King Ranch, Argentina, with the proper type and numbers of

3 See Appendix 6 for a list of the horses sent to foreign divisions of the ranch.

197

bulls immediately, we can very shortly develop purebred and crossbred sales comparable with Australia.

Therefore, we are taking the forty-nine yearling bulls that we had set aside to make selections for our 1969 auction and shipping them to Argentina to improve our breeding program. For this reason, the decision has been made that we will not hold our annual sale this year.

Demand for quality working horses in Latin America to improve the native stock is equally pressing. Since we are forced to forego our 1969 sale, we intend to utilize this opportunity to expand our horse breeding programs also. We are convinced that our decision to enlarge our Latin American production will assist purebred breeders of Santa Gertrudis cattle and American Quarter Horses everywhere by eventually opening new markets to them. Progress in this regard is evidenced by the formation of American Quarter Horse Association affiliates in Australia and Brazil. The Association has recently appointed an International Committee to act as liaison with these and other overseas organizations that form in the future.[4]

Expansion by the King Ranch continues at a rapid pace, and additions will probably continue, at least as long as Bob Kleberg is in charge. In scope, in farsightedness, in enterprise, there has never been a cattle outfit remotely comparable to the King Ranch of Texas.

[4] *Western Horseman*, December, 1968, 8–9.

32. Summary

As the old saw goes, no one legislates the kind of horse a man will breed, and no one can tell the kind of horse a man will buy. Yet breed associations exist to encourage sound breeding practices, and today people are buying more Quarter Horses than any other breed. Popular demand and common sense dictate that the Quarter Horse with the characteristics of the late nineteenth and early twentieth century must be preserved. There were and are aesthetic reasons for his preservation, but above all it is his usefulness that has made him invaluable.

Robert J. Kleberg, Dan D. Casement, and William Anson were among the first to recognize the intrinsic value of the Quarter Horse, and before 1920 all had begun to breed Quarter Horses seriously. Each did his part in encouraging the establishment of a studbook and registry. As emphasized earlier, Kleberg's breeding program was aimed at reproducing the characteristics of his stallion Old Sorrel, who in his eyes represented the ideal Quarter Horse.

I became acquainted with Bob Kleberg in 1937, when I was engaged in the organization of the American Quarter Horse Association. While I was editing the first issue of the *Stud Book and Registry,* I asked Kleberg to write a short account of the mission and place of the Quarter Horse in America. In all the intervening years no finer or more pertinent account than his has been produced. In a few short paragraphs he clearly justified

199

the breeding of Quarter Horses and explained his reasons for his conviction that they are the best horses for the rancher. Moreover, he proved to be a good prophet, for in the years since he wrote the following words the Quarter Horse has achieved all he hoped for in acceptance and popularity:

If the range livestock men of America were asked to select the horse that is the most useful for their purpose and that had contributed the most pleasure and satisfaction to their lives, I believe that they would select the Quarter Horse, or the cross of the Quarter Horse on the Thoroughbred that has retained Quarter Horse conformation. If asked to give their reasons for this choice they would say, "Our horses have to live on the range and rely on the native shrubs and grasses for their food. The Quarter Horse takes on and carries enough flesh and muscle to stand the hard work that is required of him. He has a good, quiet disposition, is easy to gentle and train, has extreme early speed and the strength and sure footedness to carry heavy weight over any kind of country. He stops and turns easily and does not become leg weary or lazy even when asked to stop and start quickly many times in the course of the day's roping, cutting, or other work.

On the average the Quarter Horse has the most symmetrical and muscular conformation coupled with the most perfect balance of any of the breeds. Good representatives of this breed are among the most beautiful of horses. Since these are the qualities desired in any type of riding horse the Quarter Horse makes an ideal foundation on which to cross the Thoroughbred or any other breed of horses used for riding.

Top cow horses are scarce and closely held. The ranchman is so jealous of these mounts that he is reluctant to see anyone but himself ride them and in only a few instances have they been allowed to leave the home ranch. For this reason their virtues are little known to the average horseman. Quarter Horses furnish the best of these and in order to preserve, increase and give the general riding public a better understanding of this wonderful breed, the American Quarter Horse Association has been formed.

The Association is very anxious to be of real benefit to the horse world. With this in mind they have chosen the most competent judges to select the mares and stallions for this, their foundation stud book. The basis of their selection at all times has been conformation and performance. They are promoting shows and contests in which the best individuals are placed.

It seems to me that from this foundation and effort the American Quarter Horse bids fair to become, or furnish the foundation for our greatest utility and pleasure riding horse. The demand for such a horse is nation wide and a very large potential demand exists throughout the world. Coming at a time when it behooves us to find new uses for our land, and contributing as it does to future national defense, the usefulness and future possibilities of this Association are very great.

The summer visits I have paid to the King Ranch have been a pleasure and a revelation. One soon learns that, as one of the older ranch employees said, "There's been a heap of living on this ranch. It's not all been just work." It has been this ability of the Kings and the Klebergs and their employees to work hard and to play hard that has prevented the constant demands of the ranch from becoming a burden. They do not have to work hard for the ranch —they want to. The ranch has been their life, from Captain Richard King down through the generations to Dick Kleberg, and now another generation is beginning to take an interest.

While no one can criticize the ranch without being straightened out, the men of the ranch are the first to laugh at themselves. I remember Bob Kleberg telling me with amusement how a visiting lady once asked him, "Need you show us the whole ranch?" This anecdote is revealing in two ways. First, it shows the pride the Klebergs have in their handiwork. Second, it demonstrates how little the guest knew about the ranch, to think that it could be seen in one visit. A worldwide organization which has been growing under the direction of three or four generations, cannot be laid out and viewed like a bedspread. It takes time and study to understand just a small part, like the Quarter Horse operations. However, it is a study well worth the time involved and rapidly becomes an experience you never forget.

APPENDICES

1. Stallions Siring Horses Used in the King Ranch Quarter Horse Program

Explanation: In the pedigree of King Ranch Quarter Horses,[1] the top line of both sire and dam always traces to the Old Sorrel. All outcross blood is found on the bottom line. In the early years many horses were brought into the program to form a nucleus for the Old Sorrel to build a breed upon, and as a safety factor to prevent genetic aberrations from occurring after the strain was begun.

The blood of most of the sires of these horses has long since been diluted, although the sires provided the vehicle upon which the strain was evolved. The Remount Service stallions shown in list 1-A were never too significant. Among the ranch-owned stallions were such sires as Lucky Mose, Martins Best and San Vicente, all of whom left their mark on the strain. The largest number of stallions is found in the Quarter Horse and half-breed lists. Many of them merely represent one parent of an unimportant female who produced one filly that entered the program. Others, such as Little Joe, made substantial contributions. These more important individuals are discussed in Chapters 20 and 21.

[1] Sources for the information given in Appendices 1 to 8 are the records and files of the King Ranch.

LIST 1. *Thoroughbred Sires of Mares*
In Quarter Horse Programs

	Birth Date			Birth Date	
A.		Remount Stallions		1933	Sudden Change
		American Flag		1934	Bim Bam
		Lion D'Or		1934	Moso
	1924	Lovely Manners		1934	Remolino
		*Naughty Boy II		1936	Don Manners
		Right Royal		1936	One Tenth
				1941	Depth Charge
B.		Ranch-owned Stallions		1943	Assault
				1947	Beau Max
		San Vicente		1947	Destino
		Lucky Mose		1947	Middleground
		Naughty Boy I		1947	On The Mark
		Naughty Boy III		1947	Poised
	1909	Martins Best		1951	High Gun
	1923	Mars		1954	Navigator
	1923	Brillante			
	1927	Boojum	C.		Other Stallions
	1933	Bold Venture			Jack Hair Jr.
	1933	Cientifico			Mokatam
	1933	Chicaro		1916	High Time

LIST 2. *Quarter Horse and Half-Breed Sires*
of Mares Used in Quarter Horse Program

	Birth Date		Birth Date
Alamo		Roan Clegg	
Bayo Gacho		Sam Watkins	
Benado		Son of Zer	
Berenge		T. T. East Dun Horse	
Black Joe*		Tarzan	
Cacahute		Tom Thumb	
Captain Jess*		Toy Boy	
Charlie Chaplin		Turtle	
Chocolate		El Unico	
Clegg Horse		Violen	
Craig Roan Horse		Yturria Horse	
Dr. Rose (Bonnie J)	1890	Texas Chief Jr.	
Dun Weathersbee Stud	1904	Ace of Hearts	
East's Yellow Jacket	1905	Little Joe	
Eligio Garcia Horse	1907	Hickory Bill	
Grano de Oro	1908	Yellow Jacket	
Horace H*	1914	Paul El	
Jiggs Jr.	1915	Oklahoma Star	
Joe Oliver*	1915	Old Sorrel	
Joe Peter	1916	Billy Sunday	
Little Hickory	1920	Magician	
Little Rex	1921	Cotton Eye Joe	
Little Tom	1923	Joe Abb	
Lucky Mose Son	1924	Jiggs	
Lupe Gonzales Horse	1925	Lone Star	
Lupe's Son	1926	Rex Beach Jr.	
McGill Horse	1927	Joe Moore	
Norias Grey Horse	1927	My Pardner	
Obregon	1930	Chicaro Bill	
Pancho Villa	1930	Lobo	
Raffles	1932	King	
Rex Beach II (Little Rex)	1935	Joe O'Brien	
Roan Canales Horse	1935	Old Man	

* Not officially listed in ranch breeding records.

Birth Date		Birth Date	
1935	Texas Star	1950	Spot Cash
1936	Del Rio Joe	1951	Bill Cresson
1936	Jack Pot	1951	Brown Tino East
1937	John Dial	1951	Dark's Colonel
1938	Old C. S.	1951	Towncrier
1939	H-Satchel Britches	1951	Wylie's Red Buck
1939	Red Head	1952	Arbolita
1941	One Eye Hippy	1952	Cactus Breeze
1944	Bill Cody	1952	Sun Tan
1944	Buck Thomas	1953	My Man
1944	Silver Wimpy	1953	Steel Bars
1945	Peppy's Ribbon	1954	Billy Kid East
1948	Morro Harrison	1954	Joe Hank
1949	Fourble Joe	1954	Poco Pine
1949	Scharbauer's King	1955	Subway
1949	Scharbauer's Pale Face	1958	Ben Bar
1950	General Lee	1958	Wimpy Deck
1950	King Troutman	1959	Wimpy Jinks
1950	Poco Tom		